What others are saying abo

Greg Asimakoupoulos has served as c[...]aplain at Co[...] the Shores for nearly a decade. During this time ne nas blessed residents and staff with his poetry, music, Bible teaching, photos and humor. Greg has provided much needed hope and support to residents and staff through the uncertain days of the coronavirus pandemic. "Sheltering in Grace" is a creative blending of COVID memories and reflections that will provide strength and encouragement for years to come.

Terri Cunliffe
President, Covenant Living Communities and Services

Experience has taught me that any time I pick up a book by Greg Asimakoupoulos, three things are going to happen: I'm going to enjoy the artistry of well-crafted poetry and articulate prose; I'm going to be surprised by insights that provoke deeper reflection and thought; and I'm going to experience the gracious presence of the God who loves me; the God who knows my heart even better than I know it; the God who goes by the name of Jesus.

Rick Lindholtz
Founder, The Pastoral Arts (a department of Artists in Christian Testimony Intl)

Much to my delight, I read these devotionals by Greg Asimakoupoulos with a growing sense of joy and enthusiasm. Greg is a wonderful writer who draws meaning out of the depths of the rich well of each day's living. His gifted creative expression and his powers of observation made this reading a delight for me — as I am certain they will for whomever else pauses with the expectation that any short moment has the potential to become surprisingly extraordinary.

Karen Burton Mains
Author and co-host of "Before We Go" podcast

During the sometimes dark and confusing days of the COVID pandemic, our community was in need of encouragement. Our chaplain, Greg Asimakoupoulos, regularly provided a timely word that offered our residents hope. I'm grateful Greg collected these devotions into this volume. They chronicle the spiritual journey at Covenant Living at the Shores and the hope we have in God.

Robert T. Howell
Executive Director, Covenant Living at the Shores

When your world is suddenly thunderstruck by an invisible villain, and now you're being told what you can and cannot do, you need a chaplain. Someone who'll help you make sense of the chaos and confinement which you most assuredly did not sign up for. Greg's love affair with words, especially God's Word, is just what the Great Physician prescribes in helter skelter days like these. Retire to your happy place and find shelter in Greg's soothing words from the Shores.

George Toles
Founder, His Deal

Sheltering in Grace is a positive and spiritual journey to help readers as they experience the daily challenges of the pandemic. Greg addresses many aspects of this new life and he gives us hope. A must read!"

Karolyn (Zuzu Bailey) Grimes
Actor in "It's a Wonderful Life"

Pastor Greg's pregame poetry has inspired Seahawks fans for many years. He has a knack for combining an optimistic view of upcoming football games with levity and the hope borne of religious conviction. Through words and actions, Pastor Greg imparts a unifying spirit binding us together. This has been especially valuable as people deal with isolation stemming from effects of the coronavirus. Pastor Greg shines as a bright beacon in the Pacific Northwest!

Mike Flood
Vice President for Community Outreach, Seattle Seahawks

Right from page one our friend Chaplain Greg Asimakoupoulos captured my heart and mind with his charming stories of life observations and spiritual growth.

Drawing, for instance, upon an imaginary conversation between God and Satan, Greg made me ask myself, "Is that what Jesus is saying to me?"

I knew I needed to enthusiastically recommend Chaplain Greg's book when he beckoned his readers to become detectives ... dusting for God's fingerprints ... suggesting that they will always find Godwinks!

SQuire Rushnell, "The Godwink Guy"
NYT Bestselling Author - Godwink Books
Executive Producer, Hallmark Godwink Movie Series

Sheltering *in* Grace
Hopeful insights in uncertain times

Greg Asimakoupoulos

Acknowledgements

I am grateful for Rick Lindholtz, a pastoral colleague and fellow author, whose expertise in independent publishing has encouraged me to keep writing. Rick's talent in design and organization finds me recommending his services to other writers. He truly is a kindred spirit.

I appreciate Joe Yakovetic's willingness to offer suggestions for the cover of "Sheltering in Grace." I first met this award-winning graphic designer at the "It's a Wonderful Life" Festival in Seneca Falls, New York. Joe designed the cover of my previous book "Zuzu's Wonderful Life." His eye for detail never blinks!

Many thanks to Barbara Krieger who was willing to proofread the manuscript. As a faithful subscriber to my weekly blog "Rhymes and Reasons," my friend, Barb, has called attention to grammar goofs and typos for the past two decades.

Mostly, I am grateful to my best friend and life companion. Since 1982 Wendy has helped me stay grounded and God-focused. My wife's encouragement and affirmation provide me with the unconditional love I need to remain creative and in-tune with the gifts God has given me.

Cover photograph by Greg Asimakoupoulos
© 2020 by Greg Asimakoupoulos

Dedication

I dedicate this volume
to the residents of
Covenant Living at the Shores,
who have modeled for me
how to shelter in grace.

Sheltering in Grace

When a crisis or virus
might cause us to fear…
we are called to abide and be still.
So we focus our faith
on the Lord's promises,
and are freed from the dread that we feel.

Abiding in Christ
means to "shelter in grace."
It's the key to remaining alive.
When we make Christ our home
and take root in His love,
we do more than just live.
We will thrive!

by Greg Asimakoupoulos

Foreword

A child, sploshing through the water after a rainstorm, noted an oil slick shimmering on a puddle just ahead of her. "Look," she squealed, "A rainbow gone to smash!"

Historians might well choose the same metaphor to describe the chaos of our time. We were a society blissfully coasting through the opening decade of the 21st century when we were hit by a perfect storm of external threat and internal division. Political differences gave way to tribalism, racial tensions gave way to violence, and ecological concerns gave way to wildfires and hurricanes. Then, out of the invisible world of epidemiology, COVID swept the globe, aggravating our conflicts and shattering our expectations. Like a rainbow gone to smash, we still see the colors of hope, but they are now blurred and shapeless images of uncertainty, if not despair.

If ever we needed daily glimpses of God's promise in the rainbow of grace, it is now. Facts that break through the despair are good, but they need the touch of song and the rhythm of poetry to put the rainbow back together again. Greg Asimakoupoulos deserves the title of "Poet Laureate" for helping us all find hope in a pandemic. With eyes wide open, he gets a glimpse of grace each day, gives it a rhyme and reason, and then offers it as a gift to each of us.

My wife, Jan, and I begin our devotions each morning by listening to Greg's daily podcast for his "sheltered" congregation at Covenant Shores. It is the best media minutes of the day. Through fresh eyes, he invites us to look for the grace in the commonplace and through rhythmic words, he makes poetic verse the joyful companion of Holy Scripture. "Sheltering in Grace" is like the old promise box on my grandma's coffee table. Each morning she would draw out a promise for the day on which she would reflect and respond. Use "Sheltering in Grace" in the same way. Read Greg's daily insights one at a time, feel the unity between prose and poetry, watch as the thoughts come alive in common duties, share the truth with others, and sense the Spirit of God showing us a rainbow of hope in a pandemic world.

David L. McKenna
President Emeritus, Seattle Pacific University

Preface

When the coronavirus first invaded our country, I was spending several days in my hometown helping my brother dismantle the family home. Several months earlier our mother died, ending a chapter in our lives that had been long in coming. Our much-loved mother had lived with dementia for a decade following our father's death. In response to Dad's request, Marc and I promised him we would not sell the home of our childhood until Mom was gone.

The task of sorting through the stuff my folks had collected living in one place more than fifty years was arduous. I realized in the midst of tossing and sorting how things we appreciate do not compare with having time with those we love. Dismantling a family home triggers precious memories of shared moments. It reminded me of how much I valued being in the presence of those people I most love. I had no idea I was about to help shepherd a group of 350 people through an extended time of forced separation from their family members.

My work in Wenatchee was interrupted by restrictions that were being put into place by our governor. Businesses and eating establishments were shut down. The senior-adult community where I am employed as a fulltime chaplain was in the process of setting strict protocols into place. The dining room was closed. Residents were asked to shelter in place. The president of our national organization requested that the chaplains at each of our twelve campuses begin producing meditations to be broadcast each day on our closed-circuit television channel.

The purpose of the daily five-minute broadcasts was to encourage individuals blindsided by a pandemic that had caught us mostly unaware. Having written a newspaper column for twenty years and having authored a dozen books during my four decades as a pastor, I had an idea. Why not collect my meditations during the season of COVID into a volume for family, friends and residents of Covenant Living? And why not call it "Sheltering in Grace"?

Obviously, the title "Sheltering in Grace" is a play on words. During COVID, we've grown accustomed to the phrase "sheltering in place" as a protocol for combating infection. It means self-quarantining. For the person of faith, sheltering in grace means to retreat to a place (literally or virtually) where we experience the protective presence of a comforting and caring God whose grace is sufficient for whatever situation in which we find ourselves. It's what the Bible refers to as abiding in Christ.

Abiding in Christ, sheltering in grace, rooted in love … that's what it takes to thrive in uncertain and scary times. Hear these words from John 15:4-5:

Abide in Me, and I in you. As the branch cannot bear fruit of itself, unless it abides in the vine, neither can you, unless you abide in Me. I am the vine, you are the branches. He who abides in Me, and I in him, bears much fruit; for without Me you can do nothing.

Abiding in Christ, sheltering in grace, rooted in love … that's what it takes to thrive in uncertain and scary times.

Sheltering in grace is what
I do when I get stressed.
I find a place where I can sense God's peace.
On a lakeside bench, beneath a tree
or shut inside my room,
I speak God's name and all my strivings cease.

God's grace is what protects me
when I'm vulnerable or scared.
Enveloped in God's arms I feel secure.
Grace is my sanctuary
where (in silence) I find hope
that no matter what may happen I'll endure.

1

Welcome to Daily Devotions. Each weekday I invite you to join me for about five minutes of inspirational thoughts intended to encourage our anxious hearts as we face the uncertainty of these unprecedented days.

It was two hundred years ago today that Frances Jane Crosby (March 24, 1820 – February 12, 1915) was born in Brewster, New York. Most of us know her by her nickname, "Fanny." During her ninety-five years of life, Fanny Crosby contributed more lyrics to our church hymnals than perhaps any other person in history.

When Fanny was six weeks old, she experienced the first of several tragedies in her life. Attempting to treat a simple eye infection, a physician used the wrong medication, leaving her permanently blind. Five months later Fanny's father died.

But her mother and grandmother instilled within the young girl a vision of a loving God who can be trusted even when we are blindsided by circumstances beyond our control.

When Fanny was eight years old, she wrote her very first poem. It was indicative of her trust in a sovereign God, her optimistic attitude toward life and her rhyming ability. Her little verse went like this:

Oh, what a happy soul I am,
although I cannot see!

I am resolved that in this world
Contented I will be.

How many blessings I enjoy
That other people don't,
To weep and sigh because I'm blind
I cannot, and I won't!

Following her graduation from the New York School for the Blind, Fanny Crosby went on to distinguish herself as a published poet and a friend of presidents, who would become the first woman to address a joint session of Congress.

Some of her more well-known hymn texts are:
    To God the Glory, Great Things He Has Done
    Blessed Assurance, Jesus is Mine
    He Hideth My Soul
    I am Thine, O Lord
    Safe in the Arms of Jesus
    Pass Me Not, O Gentle Savior

Another of Fanny's greatest hits is one that seems appropriate for where we are today in light of the COVID crisis enveloping our campus, our country and the world. And so on this, the bicentennial of Fanny Crosby's birth, hear these familiar words as if for the very first time:

All the way my Savior leads me,
What have I to ask beside?
Can I doubt His tender mercy,
Who through life has been my Guide?
Heav'nly peace, divinest comfort,
Here by faith in Him to dwell!
For I know, whate'er befall me,
Jesus doeth all things well;
For I know, whate'er befall me,
Jesus doeth all things well.

All the way my Savior leads me,
Cheers each winding path I tread,
Gives me grace for every trial,
Feeds me with the living Bread.
Though my weary steps may falter
And my soul athirst may be,
Gushing from the Rock before me,
Lo! A spring of joy I see;
Gushing from the Rock before me,
Lo! A spring of joy I see.

All the way my Savior leads me,
Oh, the fullness of His love!
Perfect rest to me is promised
In my Father's house above.
When my spirit, clothed immortal,
Wings its flight to realms of day
This my song through endless ages:
Jesus led me all the way;
This my song through endless ages:
Jesus led me all the way.

2

Through the years I've collected oxymorons. An oxymoron is a phrase of two words that seem to contradict each other. For example:

Bitter sweet
Jumbo shrimp
Act naturally
Random order
Passive aggressive
Awfully good
Civil war
Alone together

Alone together. That's what our president and our governor have called us to. Sheltering in place. Staying home in order to stay healthy. We have been instructed to remain alone. But we are not on our own in our aloneness. We are in this thing together.

Alone together. I don't like the alone part, but I am grateful for the together part. What does that old Swedish proverb say? *A shared sorrow is half a sorrow.*

In other words, experiencing hardship together even when it means being alone, makes the hardship less hard to swallow.

Alone together.
At home in community.
Distanced but not disconnected.
Holed up but not sealed off.
Quarantined but not cut off.
Shut in but not shut out.
Protected but not imprisoned.

As I think of the concept of being alone together, I'm reminded of what is true and what isn't in terms of our limited freedom and finite understanding of what is going on around us.

I'm also reminded of what the Apostle Paul wrote to his friends in Corinth. In his second letter, he reflects on God's grace in the midst of mind-numbing madness that had defined his difficult life.

For God, who said, "Let light shine out of darkness," made his light shine in our hearts to give us the light of the knowledge of God's glory displayed in the face of Christ. 7 But we have this treasure in jars of clay to show that this all-surpassing power is from God and not from us. 8 We are hard pressed on every side, but not crushed; perplexed, but not in despair; 9 persecuted, but not abandoned; struck down, but not destroyed. 10 We always carry around in our body the death of Jesus, so that the life of Jesus may also be revealed in our body. 11 For we who are alive are always being given over to death for Jesus' sake, so that his life may also be revealed in our mortal body. 12 So then, death is at work in us, but life is at work in you. (2 Corinthians 4:6-12)

In other words, we are cracked pots that leak. We are imperfect vessels that contain faith and fear, doubts and concerns, convictions and regrets. Our frailties and weaknesses as flawed human beings are quite apparent.

But lest we despair, let's look up. Or better yet, let's look in. Look in and recognize God's presence within us. The priceless treasure of God's presence is all the more visible when we humbly admit our failures and fears and look to God alone.

3

For those of us who follow the church year, this is the season of Lent. A six-week period of time when we are invited to shelter in place. It's a time to press the pause button on "business as usual." It's an opportunity to embrace the sufferings of the Savior even as we prepare ourselves for Holy Week, Good Friday and the reality of Easter Sunday.

Lent is a forty-day season that calls to mind the forty days that Moses spent on Mount Sinai when he received the Ten Commandments. For Moses, it was a time of intimacy with Yahweh with whom he related as a friend.

You will also recall that following Jesus' baptism in the Jordan River, he spent forty days in the wilderness. It was a season of reflection and temptation in which his inner spirit was being strengthened for the tasks that awaited him when he began his public ministry.

For the Christian, Lent is a season of introspection and self-examination in which our intimacy with God can be enhanced. In a way, Lent is like Advent. Advent is a quiet time of reflection that invites us to a thoughtful journey to Bethlehem and the meaning of Christ's birth at Christmas. Similarly, Lent is an invitation to prepare for the message of an empty tomb.

Five years ago my best friend here on Mercer Island died on Ash Wednesday, the beginning of Lent. That will always stand out in my mind. Ash Wednesday will forever more be linked to my friend

Ken's death.

But that's not all bad. It's the reality of death's shadow that prepares us for the incredible good news that Christ has defeated death once and for all.

This year's Lenten season will never be forgotten either. The coronavirus caused the cancelation of weekly services to which many of us have grown accustomed. One of our residents, who loves her church and its beautiful liturgy this time of the year, expressed to me how difficult it was to prepare for Easter without being able to go to her church. For her, the cancellation of services and the sheltering in place edict is a real form of suffering. I have a feeling she is not alone.

Having virtual services on Palm Sunday and Maundy Thursday and Good Friday is bad enough. But having to settle for watching Easter Sunday service on TV in your apartment? I think we'd all agree it finds us aching for what we know as normal.

There is something strangely appropriate about being denied what we are accustomed to during the Lenten season. Suffering and sacrifice go together. But so does looking beyond the suffering to the reality of redemption that yet awaits.

Hear these words from St. Paul in Romans chapter 8:

I consider that our present sufferings are not worth comparing with the glory that will be revealed in us. [19] For the creation waits in eager expectation for the children of God to be revealed. [20] For the creation was subjected to frustration, not by its own choice, but by the will of the one who subjected it, in hope [21] that the creation itself will be liberated from its bondage to decay and brought into the freedom and glory of the children of God.

[22] We know that the whole creation has been groaning as in the pains of childbirth right up to the present time. [23] Not only so, but we ourselves,

7

who have the first fruits of the Spirit, groan inwardly as we wait eagerly for our adoption to sonship, the redemption of our bodies. [24] For in this hope we were saved. But hope that is seen is no hope at all. Who hopes for what they already have? [25] But if we hope for what we do not yet have, we wait for it patiently.

[26] In the same way, the Spirit helps us in our weakness. We do not know what we ought to pray for, but the Spirit himself intercedes for us through wordless groans. [27] And he who searches our hearts knows the mind of the Spirit, because the Spirit intercedes for God's people in accordance with the will of God.

[28] And we know that in all things God works for the good of those who love him, who have been called according to his purpose. (Romans 8:18-28)

4

On March 1, we had no clue all that would transpire within a couple weeks. March Madness would be canceled. But it wasn't just the collegiate basketball playoff brackets that was called off. Schools were canceled, churches were cordoned off, restaurants and stores shuttered.

In all truthfulness, we have come to understand that March Madness means more than just college basketball. This month has been crazy! To try and flatten the curve, our lives have been altered dramatically, with recommendations we would have thought idiotic only a few weeks ago.

This morning I'd like to share with you an original poem I received in an email Sunday afternoon. (No, I'm not the only one who writes poetry!) This original verse was composed by my wife's 88-year-old mother.

Norma and my father-in-law are retired Wycliffe missionaries sheltering in place in Southern California. Each week I send them printed copies of my sermons in an attempt to encourage them as they sit on the couch at home on Sundays. Well, this Sunday she encouraged me!

Wendy's mom is quite concerned for my safety and vulnerability as I minister in my chaplain's role on the frontlines of this outbreak. After all, because of my age I am in the high-risk category when it comes to the virus.

So, in her personal quiet time she wrote this little prayer asking God to keep me and my fellow workers here at the Shores safe as we care for our residents. It's called "A Shield of Protection."

What a strange time we're in
All sequestered alone
While COVID is rampant
And we're told to "Stay home!"

But others are "out there"
Meeting germs face to face
At risk while they serve
Administering Your grace.

Oh, Father, protect!
Keep them safe from all harm;
Be a Shield of protection
In this uncertain storm.

May they rest, have assurance,
Keep them free from despair!
For you are a Shield
When they're under Your care.

Isn't that beautiful? I love the fact that it came from a senior adult who has a growing faith in God. She wants to be a blessing to those around her. She realizes she still has a purpose. The Lord wants to use you to be a source of encouragement too.

In Ephesians 6, Paul describes the armor of God – the Christian's Personal Protective Equipment. He insists that we put on this protective spiritual gear because of the dangers of the world in which we live. Paul wrote about the helmet of salvation and the sword of the Spirit and the belt of truth. But he also talks about the shield of faith. If ever we needed to access God's protective shield, it is now. The shield about which my mother-in-law writes is essential.

5

Be devoted to one another in love. Honor one another above yourselves.
[11] Never be lacking in zeal, but keep your spiritual fervor, serving the
Lord. [12] Be joyful in hope, patient in affliction, faithful in prayer. [13] Share
with the Lord's people who are in need. Practice hospitality. [14] Bless those
who persecute you; bless and do not curse. [15] Rejoice with those who
rejoice; mourn with those who mourn. [16] Live in harmony with one
another. (Romans 12:10-15)

If someone were to ask me, "So, what did you give up for Lent this
year?" I know how I would respond. The same thing we all gave
up. I gave up life as usual.

Schools are closed.
Restaurants, too.
Non-essential businesses are boarded up.
Locked beauty shops are revealing
our untouched roots.
Salons for manis and pedis are nailed shut.
Shopping malls are shuttered.
Parks are cordoned off.
So are ICU rooms.

There's no public worship.
No Lenten soup suppers.
No funerals.
AA meetings are online.
Yoga classes as well.

Sheltering in place
means we are shopping from home.
Many are working from home.
Kids are learning at home.
But there is one thing we aren't doing at home.

We aren't watching our home teams on TV at home
(or any other place).
No sports are being played.

No cruises are sailing.
Vacations have been canceled.
Wedding receptions put on hold.
Reunions as well.
And new hips will just have to wait in line
(behind new knees).

It's a Lenten season
unlike any other we've ever known.
In retrospect, giving up chocolate or meat on Fridays
doesn't seem like that big of a sacrifice anymore.
Just sayin'!

Perhaps this is the closest thing to a perfect Lent that any of us has ever known. A season where we identify with the plight of One who gave up that which He was accustomed to in order to serve the needs of those who could not save themselves.

6

We find ourselves on the frontlines of a global war as an invisible enemy advances. It is a world war that is bringing the world together instead of dividing us.

The words of Psalm 91 seem appropriate for today:

Whoever dwells in the shelter of the Most High
*   will rest in the shadow of the Almighty.*
² I will say of the LORD, "He is my refuge and my fortress,
*   my God, in whom I trust."*
³ Surely he will save you from the fowler's snare
*   and from the deadly pestilence.*
⁴ He will cover you with his feathers,
*   and under his wings you will find refuge;*
*   his faithfulness will be your shield and rampart.*
⁵ You will not fear the terror of night,
*   nor the arrow that flies by day,*
⁶ nor the pestilence that stalks in the darkness,
*   nor the plague that destroys at midday.*
⁷ A thousand may fall at your side,
*   ten thousand at your right hand,*
*   but it will not come near you.*
⁸ You will only observe with your eyes
*   and see the punishment of the wicked.*
⁹ If you say, "The LORD is my refuge,"
*   and you make the Most High your dwelling,*
¹⁰ no harm will overtake you, no disaster will come near your tent.
¹¹ For he will command his angels concerning you
*   to guard you in all your ways.*

13

Yes, the Lord is our refuge. It was true when the psalmist wrote those words. And it is true today. But, boy, this is hard. Wouldn't you agree?

I guess you'd call this
a trial separation.
Separated from family and friends
is definitely a trial.
While chats with those we love
through FaceTime, Skype and Zoom
are a blessing,
virtual visits
just aren't the same.
Digital hugs
leave my arms empty.
I want to reach out and touch
those who mean the world to me.
But, for the time being,
they are untouchables.
This trial separation
requires social distancing.

I know the day will come
when I will be separated by six feet
as the special people in my life
leave me through the door of death.
But a six-foot distance
from those with whom I work
is hard.
It's a two-yard hardship
on which we find ourselves
unwilling passengers.

And there are other ships
in this "armada of anxiety"
that are currently adrift

seeking a safe harbor
in which to anchor.
Companionship.
Friendship.
Kinship.
Worship.

7

The LORD is my shepherd;
I shall not want.
² He makes me to lie down in green pastures;
He leads me beside the still waters.
³ He restores my soul;
He leads me in the paths of righteousness
For His name's sake.
⁴ Yea, though I walk through the valley of the shadow of death,
I will fear no evil;
For You are with me;
Your rod and Your staff, they comfort me.
⁵ You prepare a table before me
in the presence of my enemies;
You anoint my head with oil;
My cup runs over.
⁶ Surely goodness and mercy shall follow me
All the days of my life;
And I will dwell in the house of the LORD forever. (Psalm 23)

Those calming words restore my soul. I'm guessing they do the
same for you. Of all the psalms tucked in the center of our Bibles,
this is the most well-known journal entry from King David's pen.

I like to think of it as the Lord's Prayer of the Old Testament. In the
Lord's Prayer (that familiar prayer that Jesus gave his followers as a
guide for how to pray), we are given a laundry list of life's concerns
in which God is involved. We are invited to ask God for divine
intervention, physical nourishment, forgiveness, guidance,

deliverance even as we celebrate being a family. Have you ever thought about that?

Because we begin the Lord's Prayer with "our Father," we are acknowledging that we are siblings (brothers and sisters) with the same Father.

The 23rd psalm also calls to mind primal human needs about which we are invited to approach our loving caring God who is likened to a compassionate shepherd.

Just think of it. Our Shepherd is concerned about our sleep and getting sufficient rest. He makes me lie down.

Our Shepherd is one who knows that beauty is key to our well-being. He makes us lie down in *green* pastures. He leads us beside *quiet waters*.

In addition, our God is keenly aware of our need for emotional and spiritual refreshment. He restores our souls.

And the psalm also points out that God is the One who guides us when we find ourselves approaching unanticipated dead ends or confusing forks in the road. He leads us for His name's sake.

As a chaplain who continually offers support to those who are in the process of packing their bags for Heaven, I am particularly grateful that this psalm deals with end of life concerns – even though we walk through the valley of the shadow of death, we will fear no evil, because the Lord is with us.

And just like the Lord's Prayer, this psalm reminds us that God is concerned with our physical need for nourishment. He prepares a table before us. Our cup overflows.

I love that this familiar psalm concludes with the assurance of goodness and mercy following us. I like to think of goodness and mercy being a couple of sheepdogs nipping at our heels keeping us on the path headed home.

How I love the 23rd psalm. It's an everyday kind of psalm that can easily be prayed at the start of the day. At the end of the day. Or anytime in between.

A resident whose husband was recently in the hospital, confessed to me that she wanted to recite some Scripture verses to her sweetheart but was drawing a mental blank. "The only thing I could think of was the 23rd psalm," she said. I assured her that beloved passage of Scripture was most appropriate.

8

Our Scripture for today comes to us from the Old Testament prophet Jeremiah. *I know the plans I have for you, declares the Lord. Plans for good and not for evil, to give you a future and a hope.* (Jeremiah 29:11)

Although we don't know how this pandemic will all play out, God knows and God has a plan. And because this worldwide crisis has not taken God by surprise, we have reason to hope.

Half a century ago, Oxford don C. S. Lewis wrote a book called *The Screwtape Letters* in which he imagined how Satan would mentor his disciples to neutralize the influence of Christianity in the world. In Screwtape Letters that mentoring took the form of letters between Satan and his novice emissary, Screwtape.

There has been a post that has gone viral on Facebook since the spread of COVID. It's attributed to C.S. Lewis, but it is merely a reflection in the spirit of the British apologist. It's a supposed dialogue between Jesus and Satan. Maybe you've read it. It's worth considering again:

Satan: *I will cause anxiety, fear, and panic. I will cause the churches to lock their doors. I will cause Christians not to worship together on Sunday. I will cause the sacraments not to be given or received.*

I will cause fights to break out at the grocery stores and on social media and inside the home. I will cause greater animosity between nations. I will cause turmoil inside and out.

Jesus: *I will restore the family. I will bring husbands and wives, mothers and fathers, sons and daughters, brothers and sisters closer together. I will greatly strengthen the communal life of religious brothers and sisters.*

I will greatly strengthen the spiritual lives of my priests. I will bring dinner back to the kitchen table and to the refectory. I will help my children slow down their lives and appreciate what really matters. I will teach my children to rely on me and not on what is of this world. I will deepen my children's faith in me. I will renew their prayer life. I will deepen their love for me and for one another.

Wow! Don't you love that? Could that be what Jesus is saying to us in the midst of this horrific pandemic?

Do you remember how our community and nation came together in the days following 9/11? I believe we are experiencing something akin to that in these days.

People are rediscovering just how much we need each other. We are being reminded what really matters in life when all is said and done.

The invisible enemy we call COVID is a common enemy in what is undeniably a world war. And yet, unlike other world wars, in this global conflict the nations are coming together as one.

9

A month ago no one could have predicted the collision course we'd be on; how our plans have been shipwrecked by circumstances beyond our control.

Speaking of shipwrecks, one of my favorite hymns was written by a Chicago lawyer whose four young daughters perished in the North Atlantic when their ocean liner collided with another ship and sunk. Horatio Spafford's wife clung to a piece of drifting debris and miraculously survived.

When Spafford learned of the tragedy, he booked passage to Europe to join his wife. The captain of the ship on which he sailed informed Spafford of the location where his daughters had drowned.

Standing at the railing of the main deck looking out over the black icy ocean, the broken-hearted father penned a poem that celebrated God's faithfulness in the midst of unthinkable sorrow. He wrote:
> *When peace like a river attendeth my way,*
> *When sorrows like sea billows roll,*
> *Whatever my lot, Thou hast taught me to say,*
> *'It is well, it is well, with my soul.'*

A little plaque with the words "It is Well with My Soul" has been sitting outside my office for the past week as a reminder of that timeless hymn and the unchanging God whose presence makes such a declaration possible.

Here are some verses from Scripture that focus our faith on the God who gives each of us the means to say "it is well with my soul."

I know the plans I have for you declares the Lord. They are plans for good and not for calamity, to give you a future and a hope. (Jeremiah 29:11)

Trust in the Lord with all your heart and lean not on your own understanding. In all your ways acknowledge Him and He will direct your paths. (Proverbs 3:5-6)

I know what it is to be in need, and I know what it is to have plenty. I have learned the secret of being content in any and every situation, whether well fed or hungry, whether living in plenty or in want. I can do all this through him who gives me strength. (Philippians 4:12-13)

Is it well with your soul? I certainly hope so. Is it well with your body? I pray for that reality as well. Is it well between you and that family member or friend with whom you've had conflict in the past?

A week that finds us shadowing our Savior (as he carried a cross to Calvary) invites us to deny ourselves, take up our cross and follow Him. To crucify our tendency to be self-sufficient, die to self and fully admit our need of Him.

What a perfect time this is (having been distanced from the people who typically populate our daily lives) to place our fears, doubts and conflicts into quarantine. Let's call a moratorium on those emotions we've allowed to control us.

Wouldn't you love to let go of your anxiety? Wouldn't you like to unload the grudge or resentment you've been carrying towards someone? Wouldn't you like to transform worry into trust?

I love a quote I read recently attributed to Corrie ten Boom: *Worry does not empty tomorrow of its sorrow, it empties today of its strength!* Isn't that great? Isn't that true? Isn't that worth taking to the bank today?

10

I sometimes like to refer to Tuesdays as "choose days." Each week I have a built-in reminder that God gave me the freedom to choose how I will act, how I will react to others, what I should believe, how much credence I should give to my feelings and to what degree I will submit my will to the Lord.

We ordinarily associate Moses with the Ten Commandments. But do you think of his successor Joshua when it comes to one equally important commandment?

Choose this day who you will serve! (Joshua 24:15)

Every day we have a choice.
Will we serve the Lord?
Or will we serve ourselves?
Will we bow before Almighty God?
Or will we pay homage to our anxiety and fear?

Today is choose day!
So let us choose wisely.

The coronavirus experts have warned us.
A week to remember awaits.
And so we face it wearing masks.

Isn't it curious that this Holy Week
could likely be a week from Hell?
Isn't it ironic that both Passover and Good Friday

will be celebrated this week?
Isn't it sobering that once again
an angel of death is passing over a nation of people
that is virtually unprepared for what is about to take place?

And for Jews and Christians alike,
this is a week that recalls
the death of a firstborn son,
the shedding of blood
and the sacrifice of a Lamb
for the atonement of those
who (by faith) make application
of what they've been instructed to do.

This is a sacred week that celebrates
the long-awaited freedom
the God of Abraham, Isaac, Jacob and Jesus
orchestrated on behalf of His people.
Freedom from tyrannical rule,
freedom from doubt
in God's power to keep His covenants,
freedom from fear of God's deserved judgment
due to our willful disobedience
and freedom from fear
associated with our inevitable death.

May this week find us grateful that a Good Friday
and an Easter Sunday make possible
a great life on earth
and an even greater life in Heaven
and the ability to trust in a God
(in the meantime)
who will not pass over
anyone who sincerely acknowledges
their need of Him.

11

Because I didn't grow up in a liturgical church, I didn't know about Maundy Thursday until I was in college. When I first heard the term, I thought of the song by The Mamas and the Papas called *Monday, Monday.*

For centuries Christians have observed Maundy Thursday (the day before Good Friday) as a time to focus on the Last Supper in the upper room and the events that took place prior to Jesus' death. In many churches there is a traditional foot-washing service as well. It's a way of reenacting that profound object lesson Jesus taught his disciples before they gathered around the table and ate their Passover meal.

Demonstrating the humility he hoped they would eventually emulate, Jesus wrapped a towel around his waist and with a basin of water, stooped before them to wash their feet. This was his way of acting out how much he loved his closest friends.

Jesus said, *Love one another as I have loved you.* He was commanding them to do for each other what they had experienced from him.

The word "maundy" is from the Latin and means "command." It's a reminder that we (like the first disciples) have been commanded to love one another like Jesus has demonstrated.

During this unusual period of time, we have been given all sorts of commands and edicts. Wash your hands. Stay at home. Wash your hands. Stay six feet apart. Wash your hands.

We understand that the marching orders we've been given are for a purpose: those who command us to observe certain behaviors are commanding a performance that has our best interest at heart. It is easier to comply with what we are asked to do when we understand the motive behind the edict.

And we understand what was in Jesus' heart that motivated his command to love each other. He said it himself: *By this will all people know that you are my disciples, by the way you love each other.* (John 13:35)

I don't know about you, but I have been blown away by the self-denying love the health workers in hospitals around the country are demonstrating. Gowned and masked, these doctors, nurses, CNAs and caregivers are putting the needs of others ahead of their own. They are obeying the Lord's command whether they realize it or not; the orders originally came from Him.

It was Jesus who also said, *Greater love has no one than this, that he lay down his life for another.* (John 15:13)

12

And we thought that 2020 would be a year that would be anything but out of focus. A 2020 vision for those who made predictions for our seemingly unstoppable economy? Hardly! A 2020 vision for those who filled out their brackets for March Madness? No way! A 2020 vision for those who pictured the best year ever to go on a cruise? What a joke!

As it turned out, the vision of these I've mentioned was comparable to Ray Charles, Stevie Wonder or Andrea Bocelli. They were blind ambitions to say the least.

Speaking of blind performers, as my wife and I watched Andrea Bocelli's Easter concert from the duomo in Milan, Wendy commented that it's a shame he can't appreciate the beauty of that breathtaking cathedral.

But what a concert he gave the world. There he was all alone (with the exception of the organist and the cameraman) in that glorious church. An empty church on Easter ... how sad! But that was not only the case where he performed; it was the norm all over the world.

Because I like to play with words and am naturally aware of the way words and phrases align (often randomly), I've been pondering the relationship between an empty tomb (the essence of the Easter message) and empty churches (the irony of this Easter season).

Some pastors in the Bible belt have taken offense that the government would dictate that congregations not gather. Some see it as a violation of First Amendment rights. Some see it as an opportunity to put personal faith ahead of patriotism, obeying a Heavenly Father rather than an Uncle Sam.

But as I've contemplated what an appropriate response would be to injunctions that limit assembling, I can't see Jesus having a problem with locking the front door of a church.

I'm convinced that
the Christ of the empty tomb
is not put off by empty churches.
After all, He has a history
of surprising His followers
who are sheltering in place
out of fear or out of necessity.
He's been known to meet up
with those who are simply
out for a walk
near their home.

Wasn't it Jesus who said,
"Where two or three
are gathered in my name,
there am I
in the midst of them"?

This Easter season, I'm especially grateful
the church is not a building
that can be locked up
or burned down.
It is a fellowship of believers
who cannot be denied
the presence of the living Lord.
The church is virtually
a family of faith.

13

This is the day the Lord has made. Let us rejoice and be glad in it. (Psalm 118:24)

And one of the reasons we can rejoice when there is still such sorrow, pain and fear in our world is the fact that our God understands our sadness and fear and is grieving along with us.

A few weeks ago Ruth Kverndal, one of our residents, shared a hymn text with me from her Lutheran hymnal. She thought it most appropriate for what we are experiencing as a community and as a nation. After reading the words, I had to agree. This hymn text that is new to me became even more meaningful when I read how the composer came to write it.

Marty Haugen wrote this meditative song during the winter of 1985-86.

Do you remember where you were on January 28, 1986? That was the fateful day the space shuttle Challenger crashed shortly after takeoff. My wife and I were in Concord, California awaiting the birth of our second child.

Marty Haugen and his family were staying at Holden Village, a retreat center at the north shore of Lake Chelan, where our neighbor, Lola Dean, has been a board member for many years.

Because communication with the outside world is infrequent at the retreat center, news of the tragedy that rocked our nation didn't reach Holden Village for a couple days.

When the facts were finally digested and sadness had blanketed the conference center, Marty picked up his pen and began to compose a hymn that would allow those at Holden to grieve along with the rest of a nation still in shock. He introduced it at an evening prayer vigil at the village. He titled his hymn, "Healer of Our Every Ill."

Marty Haugen's words provide us with a prayer for healing, not only of the body but also of the mind and spirit.

The refrain, *Give us peace beyond our fear, and hope beyond our sorrow,* is a powerful prayer and helps us express thoughts we find difficult to put into words.

You who know our fears and sadness,
grace us with Your peace and gladness,
Spirit of all comfort fill our hearts.

In the pain and joy beholding,
how Your grace is still unfolding,
give us all your vision, God of love.

Give us strength to love each other,
every sister, every brother,
Spirit of all kindness be our guide.

You who know each thought and feeling,
teach us all Your way of healing,
Spirit of compassion, fill each heart.

And then the refrain:

Healer of our every ill.
Light of each tomorrow,
give us peace beyond our fear
and hope beyond our sorrow.

14

Most of you are old enough to remember listening to the events of World War 2 while gathered around the family radio in the living room.

The family radio and newsreels at the local theater were the means by which Americans were informed as to what was going on in the world. Oh, how times have changed. Now cable news networks on our televisions tempt us to watch the events of the pandemic-plagued planet 24/7. The internet gives news junkies their hourly fix on a smartphone.

There are times when I wish that all we had was the family radio and the simplicity of life that receiver represented.

I have radio on my mind today. And for good reason. Sixty years ago a radio station in Nome, Alaska went on the air for the very first time. It was the only means of providing villages on the Bering Sea with news, information, entertainment and religious programming.

This radio station just south of the Arctic Circle proved to be a lifesaving station for those needing to communicate messages to family members announcing the births of grandchildren or the deaths of elders. When fish camp would open. When the flight with groceries would arrive. When the traveling doctor would be in town.

Because of the long dark arctic winters of Nome, the Evangelical Covenant denomination (that operated the new venture) gave the radio station most appropriate call letters. KICY.

In 1960, April 17 fell on Easter Sunday, a most appropriate day to go on the air with the good news of the Gospel. K-*ICY* would warm the hearts of lonely villagers struggling with depression, alcoholism and unemployment.

Soon it was discovered that the signal crossed the Bering Sea and could be heard in the Russian Far East. So, Russian language programs were produced to share God's love with those for whom grace was a foreign concept.

Today, KICY broadcasts good news as well as national and international news to those who want to be reminded that God has the whole world in His hands.

My wife and I and our daughters had the privilege of working at KICY the summer of 1987. I was so impressed by what I witnessed, I wrote a book chronicling the history of this amazing radio station some years later. The book is called *Ptarmigan Telegraph*.

Our text for today is a most appropriate one:

How beautiful on the mountains are the feet of those who bring good news, who proclaim peace, who bring good tidings, who proclaim salvation, who say to Zion, 'Your God reigns!' (Isaiah 52:7)

This week, against the backdrop of ongoing bad news, we all need some good news. We need to hear messages of peace that remind us that the God we worship really does reign.

15

Speaking of marathons, yesterday was Patriot Day in Boston and as you probably know, that is the day when the annual Boston Marathon is run each year. But not this year! Runners from all over the world (who had trained and had qualified for this most famous of all marathons) were stopped in their tracks.

As the poet has been known to say,
There can be no race
when you're having to shelter in place.

I wonder if disappointed Bostonians decided to have a virtual tea party instead?

All the same, you and I find ourselves in a marathon that hasn't been canceled. We are doing all that we can to put one foot in front of the other each day. The marathon to which I'm referring is called life.

Like the athletic version, the marathon of life is a long haul. There is a change of scenery along the way. Each mile has its unique challenges. Different stretches of the course have different characteristics. Some have beautiful landscapes and others are rather nondescript. Some are more joyful and others are more difficult.

In the Boston Marathon there is an especially hard section of the race. It begins about mile 20 and includes a steep incline. It's known as Heartbreak Hill. Runners have to pace themselves if they intend to complete what they've started.

In our marathon we find ourselves at a very challenging milepost. We've been sheltering in place for months. We've had limited exposure to people we care about deeply. Our familiar routines have been hugely altered. A low-grade fear (mostly asymptomatic) has infected our peace of mind.

But like those runners in the Boston Marathon who reach mile 20, we need to pace ourselves and commit to doing what we can to gear up for what's ahead. Let's not expect more than is realistic. Let's be honest. Let's admit this is hard. This is boring. This is taxing our nerves. This is draining our creative energy.

But we need to remember that our Heartbreak Hill (just like the one in Bean Town) isn't non ending. Life will level out.

I don't know about you, but I find encouragement from Hebrews 12:

Therefore, since we are surrounded by such a great cloud of witnesses, let us throw off everything that hinders and the sin that so easily entangles. And let us run with perseverance the race marked out for us, fixing our eyes on Jesus, the pioneer and perfecter of faith.

16

I'm a big fan of Godwinks.

Godwinks are those seemingly random occurrences that we often call coincidences. It could be an answered prayer or maybe simply an experience that evokes the response, *Wow, what are the odds of that?!* They are unanticipated connections that we can't explain.

The term Godwinks was coined a number of years ago by a former ABC TV television executive by the name of SQuire Rushnell with whom I've recently started to correspond.

SQuire explains Godwinks this way:

Think about when you were a kid and someone you loved gave you a little wink across the dining room table ... Mom or Dad or Grandma. You didn't say, "What do you mean by that?" You knew.

It meant: "Hey kid, I'm thinking about you right now." A Godwink is a message of reassurance from above, directed to you. It's a way God says, "Out of seven billion people on the planet, I'm thinking of you! Keep the faith! You're never alone."

SQuire believes (and I tend to agree) that Godwinks occur in our lives more than we realize. And if that's true, we should be looking for evidence of God's presence in our lives on a daily basis.

David and Karen Mains, with whom I used to work, wrote a book several years ago called *The God Hunt*.

Their premise is similar to SQuire's. They contend that God leaves evidence of His presence at unexpected times and in unanticipated places and we just need to be on the lookout. David and Karen Mains are convinced that we can learn to dust for God's fingerprints in our lives much like an evidence-seeking detective.

So how about it? Are you willing to go on a God Hunt with me today in search of Godwinks? In Romans chapter 8 the apostle Paul celebrates a gift God has given to all His children. It's the promise that God is sovereignly involved in the events that occur in our lives. He writes: *All things work together for the good of those who are called according to God's purpose.* (Romans 8:28)

Wow! Isn't that great news? God causes all things to work together for His purpose in our lives. What a great thought with which to begin today. Wait! Was that a wink I just saw?

17

I've been thinking about the difference packaging makes when it comes to delivering an important message. Truth can be delivered in different containers. And when push comes to shove, containers make all the difference in the world.

When push comes to shove
soon the gloves will come off
and what started as shoves become fists.
But bare-knuckled brawling's
the last thing we need.
Am I right? Yes, I am. I insist!

What needs being said
can be said in two ways.
The truth can be pushy or kind.
When we're pushed, we push back.
But, when loved, we perk up.
To the facts offered harshly, we're blind.

Over the last several weeks I (with you) have watched a lot of those coronavirus press conferences from the White House. Some of the presenters are easy to listen to and informative while others are hard to handle and off-putting.

And then there is Dr. Anthony Fauci. What a guy! Don't you just love him? All five-feet-six of him. My wife and I watched a documentary over the weekend about the 1918 flu pandemic made a decade ago. Who should be interviewed in it but Dr. Fauci? It's a fascinating program available on YouTube.

Anyway, it was fun to see a much-younger Dr. Fauci. There's just something about his style. He doesn't pull any punches. He is straight-forward. Like Joe Friday, just the facts, ma'am. He tells the truth.

But the way he says it doesn't turn you off. Maybe it's his smile. Maybe it's his chronically hoarse, gravelly voice. Or maybe it's the fact that he cares about those he's talking to. He speaks the truth in love.

Speaking in the truth in love... Did you know that is a biblical concept? It's found in Ephesians 4:15.

And it's a timeless concept that is worth its weight in gold. Framing the way we convey our facts may take a bit more of our time, but the outcome is worth the effort. The container in which we package our words can sometimes drown out what we want to say.

So let's be mindful of how we communicate. Let's be disciples of St. Anthony Fauci.

18

We can choose to greet this day gratefully or we can choose to collide with this day critically. That's why I call it Choose-day!

I have an amazing mother-in-law. Norma will be ninety on her next birthday. Would you believe she still writes curriculum for a weekly Bible study she leads in Southern California? She was raised in a very conservative closed Plymouth Brethren congregation where women were not allowed to participate. But she went on to become an elder in the Presbyterian church. This retired missionary with Wycliffe Bible Translators is a published author and poet.

Last week she sent me a poem she'd written in her early morning quiet time. She calls her poem, "Joy in Trouble." It's based on The Epistle of James 1:2-4 where the Apostle encourages us to maintain a positive perspective when faced with perplexing times.

In this pandemic of 2020,
It's hard to understand
That God can use these "troubles,"
Spread across our land,

To perfect and help us grow
In endurance, self-control,
Giving joy, filling needs,
Making life complete and whole.

Oh, may we learn the lessons
God is giving every day
And not waste this hard intrusion
That has come, it seems, to stay.

*Lord, develop our **endurance**,*
May we give it room to grow
Until we are made perfect
Needing nothing – complete and whole!

I've always liked the passage on which Norma based her poem. I especially like James 1:2-4 as translated by the New Testament scholar J.B. Phillips:

When all kinds of trials and temptations crowd into your lives, don't resent them as intruders, but welcome them as friends!

Realize that they come to test your faith and to produce in you the quality of endurance. But let the process go on until that endurance is fully developed.

Well, our faith (as well as our patience) has been tried over the past several weeks. But the key to "welcoming such trials as friends" is perspective. Will we choose to trust as we continue to be inconvenienced? Or will we choose to complain?

On this Choose-day, that choice is up to you.

40

19

You know what isn't fun? The skin-cancer treatment I've been enduring for the past six weeks. It has left my face looking quite sunburned. But it's not a sunburn. It's a chemical burn that has intentionally irritated my face. The purpose is to identify pre-cancer cells and burn them off.

One of the blessings of going through this treatment now is the fact that I've had to wear a face covering anyway. This morning I am counting my blessings that my treatment is finished as of today.

During the past month and a half I could easily have questioned if the cure is worse than the disease I'm trying to avoid. That's an expression we've heard related to the coronavirus pandemic. Is the cure worse than the disease? The measures we've endured attempting to flatten the curve certainly have exacted a toll.

At times it has seemed that the price tag trying to avoid infection is greater than the price tag associated with the virus.

But it's at times like this when we need to remind ourselves that often the outcome we long for (though costly) is well worth the process. It's like refining precious metals.

The apostle Peter describes this process in his first epistle. He says if we want to grow and mature in our faith walk, there is no escaping the face-scraping pain of suffering. Suffering is inevitable if we want to reach our potential as followers of Christ. And Peter says we can actually reach a point of rejoicing in the process as painful as it is:

In all this you greatly rejoice, though now for a little while you may have had to suffer grief in all kinds of trials. ⁷ These have come so that the proven genuineness of your faith – of greater worth than gold, which perishes even though refined by fire. (1 Peter 1:7)

The inconveniences connected to the coronavirus are part of the process God is using to strengthen our trust in Him. Our faith is punctuated by the personal trials we face. While our tendency is to draw back from the heat of the fire, let's ask God for the ability to face the flame and trust the process.

That health issue you're dealing with? That family member you're concerned about? That anxiety that is holding you hostage? Give it to the Lord.

20

Our vision for 2020 back in January proved to be more nearsighted than we could have imagined.

Our focus on the coronavirus finds us bleary eyed and not able to see straight as we anticipate how all this is going to play out.

Fortunately some things are changeless. Take Mount Rainier for instance. It towers over the Puget Sound region with grace and majesty. Whenever that 14,000-foot ice-cream-shaped volcano is visible, it brings me joy.

I can remember as a ten-year-old kid going to Seattle Rainier baseball games at Sick's Stadium. As my dad maneuvered the car from Highway 99 to Boren Avenue and then on to Rainier Avenue, the mountain seemed to stand on tip toe to take a bow. Seeing the mountain close up meant we were almost to the stadium.

Over the years Mount Rainier has helped me to understand the presence of God in my life and in our world. There are days (most days actually) when Mount Rainier is not visible. But does that mean that the mountain is not there? Absolutely not! The mountain stands tall and fortress-like all the time.

The fact that low-lying clouds keep us from seeing what's behind them or above them does not negate the reality of the mountain's presence. Neither does my inability to detect God's presence mean God is nowhere to be found.

When I moved to Pasadena, California back in 1976 to attend Fuller Seminary, I was pleased by my professors and the courses I was taking. But I was not happy about the poor quality of the air.

Half a century ago, the smog in the LA basin was abysmal. Would you believe I lived in Pasadena for two weeks before I realized the "city of roses" was nestled up against the San Gabriel Mountains?

Like Mount Rainier, the San Gabriel Mountains were a permanent fixture of the geographical area. My inability to see them didn't negate their existence.

Sometimes we struggle to see God in the midst of our daily lives. He's hidden from view. Our eyes sting from the pollutants of unanswered prayer or the way God answers our prayers differently than we hoped.

There are storm clouds on the horizon of our lives that block us from seeing God at work. When the sky is dark from a doctor's diagnosis, a family member's divorce or the unexpected death of a friend, we fixate on what we are blindsided by.

But, just like Mount Rainier, God is there. Whatever keeps us from seeing Him does not (cannot) remove Him from our lives.

I love the words St. Paul penned that are recorded in Romans 8: *I am convinced that nothing can separate us from the love of God that is in Christ Jesus.* (Romans 8:39)

And do you know what the root word translated *nothing* means? It means NOTHING. Nothing can separate us from God's love or God Himself. Because He is always there.

GODISNOWHERE   GOD IS NOWHERE?   GOD IS NOW HERE!

21

And after six weeks of experiencing a new definition of "camping" on campus, we all need a little humor to help us over the hump.

So, what do you call a camel that has no humps? Of course. His name is Humphrey.

What day did I say it was? Right! It's May the 4th.

And maybe your grandkids (like my grown kids) have fun with this day. If they're Star Wars fans, they probably do.

There's that famous line from that memorable movie: *May the Force be with you!*

May the 4th be with you. Get it?

Well, one thing I hope you get is the fact that God is with us. Although these dramatic efforts to flatten the curve and minimize infection and death during this pandemic find us more alone than we are accustomed to, we are not entirely alone. We are alone together. We are physically distant but not socially distant.

But we are not entirely alone for an entirely different reason. God is with us in our aloneness.

My favorite name for Messiah is IMMANUEL. God with us! The foundational truth of the doctrine of incarnation is that the Creator emptied Himself of His divine prerogatives in order to fill the human frame of a finite creature.

In other words, God became like us and lived among us to tangibly demonstrate for us that He is with us. That we are not alone. That we are never alone.

That the holy infinite Almighty One understands our plight as passengers on an imperfect spaceship hurdling through the cosmos because He has been a fellow passenger.

Yesterday Christians around the globe celebrated the fourth Sunday of Eastertide. In other words, we are still embracing the truth that death has been defeated and that because it has been defeated there is nothing, absolutely nothing that can separate us from God's love or His presence.

From an empty tomb we hear the echoing voice of God: *I will never leave you or forsake you.* Can you imagine Him saying it to you? *I will never leave you or forsake you.* (Hebrews 13:5)

I can only imagine. Can you? Immanuel. God with us, indeed.

May the force of God's unstoppable love be with you because He is with you.

22

My wife grew up in Mexico City as a missionary kid. As such she has educated me about Mexican culture over the 38 years we've been married. You should hear Wendy sing the Mexican National Anthem. It should come as no surprise to you that we have tacos at our house on a regular basis.

Most people think Cinco de Mayo is Mexican Independence Day. It actually isn't. It celebrates a successful battle waged in the State of Puebla during the French and Mexican War.

Would you believe that Cinco de Mayo is a more popular celebration in the United States than it is in Mexico? The "5th of May" gained momentum in our country as Hispanics found an opportunity to celebrate their ethnic identity. Chicano activists raised awareness of the holiday in the 1960s, in part because they identified with the victory of indigenous Mexicans over European invaders during the Battle of Puebla.

Celebration of one's ethnic origins calls to mind the multifaceted diversity of the Kingdom of God. Followers of Christ are found in every continent of the globe. They look different and dress different and express their worship differently. The church is a colorful tapestry comprised of beautiful threads woven together by God's grace.

I love the picture we are given in the last book of the Bible that describes the heavenly celebration at the end of time. In Revelation 7:9 it says:

After this I looked, and there before me was a great multitude that no one could count, from every nation, tribe, people and language, standing before the throne and before the Lamb. They were wearing white robes and were holding palm branches in their hands.

Our residents represent a wonderful conglomerate of heritages including British, Italian, German, Finnish, Filipino, Latvian, Chinese, Japanese, Romanian, Indian, Greek, Hungarian, Danish, Dutch, Norwegian, Swedish, Kenyan, Russian, Irish and Scottish. But that kind of diversity in not unique to our community.

How about we make note of our own ancestral heritage and thank God for the fact that He is Lord of all? Whether we eat enchiladas and tacos or lefsa and lutefisk, let's thank God for the unique dish we represent at His potluck.

23

Welcome to yet another day in your wonderful life. You see, George Bailey isn't the only person who can admit to having a wonderful life (in spite of trials, tribulations and coronavirus complications that derail our comfortable routines).

I have a working hypothesis that if we're honest, the profit/loss printout of our life experiences show more things to be grateful for than things to gripe about.

Some years ago, while preparing to speak at the annual *It's A Wonderful Life* film festival in upstate New York, I wrote this little rhyme:

It's a wonderful life even though it's been tough
with the hardships and heartaches we've faced.
Our blessings outnumber
what's brought us much pain
when we look back at times we were graced.

It's a wonderful life if we choose to believe
that our lives have touched others for good.
Through the words that we've said
or the deeds we have done
we've brought joy to the world (as we should).

It's a wonderful life we've been given by God.
What George Bailey discovered is true.
Every day is a gift

to unwrap and enjoy
while acknowledging someone needs you.

I'm convinced that the key to maximizing the joy factor in our daily lives is identifying where we can serve someone else and then actually responding in a tangible way with acts of kindness.

Jesus went public with his mission statement early in his ministry. It's recorded in Mark 10:45. I memorized it when I was a freshman in college taking an underclass New Testament course: *For the Son of Man did not come to be served but to serve and to give his life as a ransom for many.*

Our sheltering-in-place restrictions limit our service options right now. But reaching out to others in need does not require physical touch.

You can touch someone with a text or an email acknowledging your concern for what a family member or friend is going through. You can express empathy for someone who is experiencing a loss that you know all too well. A FaceTime visit or a phone call can lift the spirits of another who is really struggling with loneliness or cabin fever. You might consider sending a little money to a grandchild who has been laid off from their job. Or baking a batch of cookies for the frontline staff in a local nursing home.

That's not an exhaustive list by any means. But maybe those are some suggestions to get you thinking about how to serve someone else going through their own personal challenges in this very universal challenging time.

24

Years ago I wrote a poem called *A May Prayer* to celebrate the month of May. But as you can easily see, it applies to any month of the year.

May you discover in this month
that Easter's not a day,
but rather it's a way of life
by which faith learns to play!

May you experience the joy
just knowing Jesus lives!
May you not fear what's still to come
but trust a God who gives.

May you determine to give thanks
for all that's going right.
May you look past another's wrong
so you'll sleep well at night.

May you dust for God's fingerprints
in all that springtime brings:
a flow'ring shrub, a fragrant rose,
the tune a songbird sings.

May you decide to make a friend
of someone you don't know.
May you mend frayed relationships
although you cannot sew.

May you delight in getting fit
by walking every day.
May you eat what is good for you
and chart how much you weigh.

May you take time to talk to God
and then to contemplate
the ways the Lord has answered prayer
with "Yes" or "No" or "Wait!"

May you begin each day this month
by reading from God's Word
and listening expectantly
for what the ancients heard.

May you unwrap each day as if
the present is a gift.
And may God's presence grant you peace
and give your soul a lift.

25

Today I'd like to honor our nurses and Certified Nurse Assistants. This is, after all, Nurse Appreciation Week.

In the skilled-nursing wing of our campus, there is a colorful banner in the hallway expressing our communal gratitude. There is also a big beautiful sign at the entrance to our property that announces HEROES WORK HERE. I love that!

As part of Nurse Appreciation Week, we held a "Blessing of the Hands" ceremony for our nursing staff. It was an opportunity for me as chaplain to anoint the hands of each caregiver and consecrate them. It was a tangible way to help each nurse see their hands as an extension of the healing hands of God.

As they lined the hallway (socially distanced), they held out their hands as I prayed on their behalf:

Please bless these hands that they may be
more than gloved fingers others see
but channels of Your healing love
that comfort with their touch.

And may these hands of mine be Yours
who see the sacred in their chores
while reaching out both day & night
with gratitude and joy.

So as I fold these hands in prayer

convinced You'll use them as I care
for precious people needing me,
I hold on for dear life.

Hands are important. Fingerprints identify us as unique individuals. Fingers are the original digital calculator. We learn to count on our fingers when we are preschoolers.

But hands signify the personal power of touch. Jesus touched those whom he healed. The power of personal touch. The right hand historically was considered a symbol of honor.

Hands are important on a number of levels. We hold hands. We clap our hands. We raise our hands. We wash hands. Do we ever!

We use our hands to write, to cook, to make our beds, to type, to wash dishes. We use our hands to tossel a toddler's hair or cradle a newborn.

Hands down, we value our hands. And God does too. When we give God our hands, we can use them as an act of worship and service.

26

Do you know what else tends to complicate our lives? Celebrating Mother's Day when you don't have a mother any more. How do you go about it? What do you do?

I'm open to your suggestions. I'm all ears. Since my mom passed away last summer, this is my first Mother's Day with no one to call, visit or send to a card to.

Honoring my wife (the amazing mother of our three grown kids and the incomparable Nana to our two granddaughters) is one way to observe Mother's Day. Celebrating our married daughter, who is an incredible mom to Imogen and Ivy, is another way to mark this Mother's Day. I look forward to honoring both these awesome moms. But Wendy's not my mom and Allison's not my mom.

Those of you who lost your mom to death years ago, how do you do it? What can you teach me?

Do you flip through old family photo albums and make a mental movie of priceless memories? Speaking of movies, do you watch old family videos in which your mom is prominently featured? Do you recreate a meal your mom used to make by following her time-tested family recipe? What do you do?

It's possible that after all these years even you are struggling to find appropriate ways to honor your mom's memory. How about writing her a letter recounting the many ways she influenced your life?

COVID has left undermined our normal ways of doing things. You could write a prayer thanking your Heavenly Father for the part your mother played in forming your faith. What about penning an original poem highlighting her unique characteristics?

According to Scripture there is yet another way to honor our mothers. One of my favorite passages from which to preach on Mother's Day is the text found in John 19:27. (Ironically, 1927 the year my mom was born.)

In that passage we find Jesus hanging on the cross, dying in our place as the perfect sacrifice for a sinful planet. While struggling to breathe, the Savior observes his grieving mother standing at the foot of the cross. Concerned for her well-being, he calls to one of his disciples. With his ebbing strength he asks John to care for his mom after he's gone. *Behold your mother!,* Jesus groans.

In other words, Jesus is redefining family relationships for those who are his followers. John is called to love Mary as if she were his mother.

Bingo! There's yet another way to spend Mother's Day. Following Jesus' example, we can expand our horizon of those who are deserving and show tangible appreciation for those mothers who are grieving for the loss of their children or their husbands.

Who might be a surrogate mother to whom you could show honor this year and in the process honor the one who introduced you to Jesus when you were just a child? Who is a woman in your sphere of influence who needs to be reminded that her life matters, no matter the challenges she currently faces? What might you do to comfort her?

27

I don't know about you, but I am really enjoying these daily points of contact. Just a few minutes each morning to focus beyond the headlines of the front page. It's a reality check. It's an opportunity to expand the parameters of our perspective and lengthen our horizon. In other words, it's a chance to look up and look in and allow our faith to focus.

Remember that playground rhyme from the time we were kids? One would give the orders and we would dutifully obey. *Look up! Look down! Look at my thumb!* And the dictator would say, *Gee, you're dumb.*

When we look up at God and look down inside our hearts, we aren't dumb at all. What was it the Scriptures say? *The fear of God is the beginning of wisdom.*

This past week my monthly article appeared in our local newspaper. In this newest column I reflected on life lessons rooted in the COVID pandemic.

As I've reflected on the checklist of behaviors we've been given to flatten the curve and stop the spread of COVID, I realized such instructions relate to more than just this virus. Against the backdrop of this health crisis, I've been reminded of timeless life lessons.

For starters, consider *Remember to wash your hands.* In addition to the hygienic benefits of literally scrubbing our digits for twenty seconds, there is symbolic value.

Historically speaking, "washing your hands" of a given situation means putting something behind you. Remember in the Gospel account of the weekend Jesus was crucified, he was brought before Pontius Pilate to be interrogated.

Pilate, the Roman governor of Judea, couldn't find sufficient reason to execute the Galilean rabbi. But the crowd insisted on Jesus being sentenced to death. And what did Pilate do? He obliged the blood-hungry crowd and ordered crucifixion. But then he washed his hands of his responsibility. He put it behind him.

That's kind of a negative illustration of the power of washing one's hands. But it makes the point, right?

Washing our hands of the past can have positive ramifications for us as well. Too often we hang on to regrets of the past we can't do anything about. We need to learn to forgive ourselves. Christianity celebrates the concept of grace. And grace allows us to follow Princess Elsa's lead and "let it go!"

What do you need to wash your hands of today?

St. Paul is the one who wrote, *But this one thing I do: Forgetting what is behind and straining toward what is ahead,* [14] *I press on toward the goal to win the prize for which God has called me heavenward in Christ Jesus.* (Philippians 3:13)

28

Social distancing has become a new addition to our English vocabulary. We've been told that maintaining a six-foot distance can prevent unnecessary burials six feet under. And we've done a good job at it for the most part. But the whole concept of social distancing speaks to me of the importance of *giving each other space*.

It is important to give those with whom we interact the freedom to espouse and act on their own perspective. Insisting others see things "our way" crowds creativity and selfishly suffocates.

I know someone has said that if two people agree about everything, then one of them is unnecessary. But the New Testament illustrates how God uses people who approach life differently to accomplish His purposes.

Paul and Barnabas disagreed about their traveling companion and went their different ways. Paul and Peter had differing views when it came to how they communicated the essence of the faith.

Paul recognized that he was a good church planter but not the best at staying for the long haul. Apollos was better suited for that. Get it? Giving each other space to do what we are gifted to do and giving each other the freedom to express our perspective promotes healthy relationships in the Body of Christ.

God has given us personal space in the gift of each day. I rather like the term *24-hour capsule of time*. My friends working the 12 steps of AA celebrate the importance of living life one day at a time.

And if God has seen fit to give us space to express our free will, we would do well to follow His lead and give one another personal space and privilege to express our values and opinions.

Believing that today is your very own personal space, with what will you fill this capsule of time? Reading? Researching genealogical clues through Ancestry.com? Watching TV? Writing a chapter of your family history? Sewing face coverings? Going for a walk by the lake with a friend (six feet apart)?

My dad often recited a poem that celebrated the time capsule we call today. Perhaps you've heard it.

The clock of time is wound but once
and no one has the power
to tell just when the hands will stop
at late or early hour.

Now's the only time you own,
so love and toil with will.
Tomorrow the hands will finally stop
forever to be still.

29

In our state the governor has instructed us to stay home to stay healthy. And sheltering in place has largely accomplished that goal. In the process, however, we have rediscovered the value of balance in our lives.

If we're honest I think we'd have to admit the "old normal" of daily life found us in the prime of our lives spending too much time at work and investing in pursuits that took us away from our families.

Having rebooted our home page, I'm hoping the "new normal" will find our adult children and grandchildren who are still in the work force recognizing the importance of staying home more often.

Home represents that place where we recharge our batteries. But it's more than that. It's the place where we center down and remember that God created us to be human beings more than humans doing. Home is where we find our primary identity as a person unconditionally loved. It's a place where our worth is based on who we are 24 hours a day, not on what we accomplish in a 40-hour work week.

Our Jewish neighbors typically have a miniature rectangular metal box attached to the door frame of their home. It's called a *mezuzah*. It contains sacred words from Deuteronomy 6 where God has commanded His people to see the home as the primary space from which faith is nurtured and passed on and where He is honored.

Even at this stage of our lives, our homes are sacred places. Where we spend most of our time is holy ground. So this current requirement to shelter in place is not all that bad. It's a forced reminder that staying home has its benefits.

Staying home helps us stay focused on what really matters. Or as the title of a book by one of my favorite authors intimates, "Home is where life makes up its mind."

Recently Kathleen Parkinson, one of our residents, shared with me a poem by Kitty O'Meara that went viral on social media:

And the people stayed home.
And read books, and listened, and rested,
and exercised, and made art, and played games,
and learned new ways of being, and were still.
And listened more deeply.
Some meditated, some prayed, some danced.
Some met their shadows.
And the people began to think differently.
And the people healed.
And, in the absence of people living in ignorant,
dangerous, mindless, and heartless ways,
the earth began to heal.
And when the danger passed,
and the people joined together again,
they grieved their losses, and made new choices,
and dreamed new images,
and created new ways to live and heal the earth fully,
as they had been healed.

30

As you know, I've been contemplating life lessons derived from the directives the coronavirus task force has been giving us. These prescribed behaviors invite us to do more than simply take the requirements at face value.

Today I'm pondering the importance of *wearing a mask.*

It appears that face coverings will be part of our daily wardrobe for the foreseeable future. It appears to be the "new normal." My Seahawks mask will allow me to express my allegiance as a "12" on more than just Blue Fridays. It will also provide others with protection should I unknowingly transmit a virus that finds me asymptomatic.

Wearing a mask when it comes to the current pandemic prevents us from infecting someone close to us with the droplets we might deposit in the air from a cough or a sneeze (or even singing a song).

But there are also times in life when it is most appropriate to wear a different kind of mask as well. I'm referring to an invisible mask. In other words, covering up for the sake of another.

I'm thinking of those times when another's painful situation calls us to hide our personal emotions. In such settings we are not denying our own plight. Rather, masking our issues allows us to focus on the needs of someone else that are more critical at the moment.

Don't you hate it when you share a painful experience in your life only to have the person with whom you are sharing it one-up you with something similar they've experienced? What you needed was someone to hear your heart and feel your pain. Instead, what you got was someone attempting to compete with your level of angst.

In Galatians 6:2 the apostle Paul calls us to *bear one another's burdens and so fulfill the law of Christ.*

Keeping our mouths shut while opening our ears to hear someone's personal suffering is a way we bear their burden. Because we mask our own sorrow so not to compete with theirs, it's a burden for us as well. But it's a burden we gladly bear in order to express love the way Jesus loves us.

As someone much wiser than I once observed, *There is a reason God gave us two ears and one mouth. We are supposed to listen twice as much as we speak.*

31

Today's life lesson from the coronavirus restrictions relates to how we gather in times of a pandemic. I would title this lesson *Meet up creatively*.

Back when I was a kid, Zoom was a hot cereal. Not anymore. Those Brady Bunch screenshots we've been seeing are everywhere. You see them on your computer and on your virtual worship services and on the news.

Gratefully, social distanced does not mean being socially disconnected. As human beings, we are created for community.

The beginning chapters of our Bible inform us that we were created in the image of God. Ours is a God who said (in the plural): *Let US create humankind in OUR image*. If the Creator was in community (as Father, Son and Holy Spirit) and if we are created in that image of community, we demand community or we die.

No wonder the writer of the letter to the Hebrew Christians that is contained near the end of our New Testaments wrote, *And do not neglect meeting together as some are in the habit of doing*. (Hebrews 10:25). The person who wrote those words understood how critical it was for Christ-followers to maintain fellowship in order to flourish.

As I implied before, we are social animals. And even when it seems like this zoo-like reality finds us seemingly confined in cages, we need others to look at. We need others to talk to. We need others to listen to.

We can't help but find ways to interact. Even though we are sheltering in place alone, we take comfort that we are alone together. More than that, we find ways to comfort one another by reaching out.

In sickness and in health, we are social beings who cannot neglect the assembling of ourselves albeit creative.

Bottom line? We virtually cannot live without each other. And gratefully we are finding ways to connect virtually. Companies are conducting virtual staff meetings. Churches are congregating remotely. My musician daughter is teaching flute lessons via Skype and my youth pastor son-in-law is interacting with students via FaceTime. Don't you love the video clips we see on the nightly news of drive-by birthday parties and balcony concerts in apartment complexes? And we can be creative in connecting with God, too.

Take a few minutes to contemplate how to approach prayer creatively. If prayer is primarily engaging God with your thoughts and emotions, what might you do today to communicate with the Creator?

32

In the 90th Psalm, Moses asks the Lord for help with homework. Back when I was in school, I needed help with homework, too. Especially with math. And that's the subject for which the Prince of Egypt needed assistance too.

Teach us to number our days, he asks. *Teach us to number our days that we might gain a heart of wisdom.* (Psalm 90:12)

One way to number our days is to recall the days of our lives that have specifically proved meaningful and reflect on the lessons they call to mind.

April 15, 1912 was the day the Titanic sunk. A day that proved that it's the little things in our lives that can take us under if left unheeded. The ship's collision with that notorious iceberg resulted in hairline cracks that caused the fatal outcome of a ship "not even God could sink." It was not an obvious wound to the body of the vessel that claimed her life.

November 22, 1963 was the day Camelot ended for America's royal family on a motorcade through Dallas. We all can recall where we were when we heard that President Kennedy had been gunned down. It was a trip the president had been warned not to take. It's a day that reminds us of the importance of heeding the advice of those we trust.

July 20, 1969 was the day Neil Armstrong voiced those memorable words from the surface of the moon: *One small step for man, a giant leap for mankind.* It was a day we recognized that not all impossible dreams really are.

September 11, 2001 was the day Mother Liberty looked on in horror as her twin towers collapsed at her feet. It was a day we discovered that even the greatest nation on God's green earth is vulnerable to tyranny and terrorism on our home soil.

And let's not forget May 18, 1980. That was the day when a majestic mountain named for a peaceful saint exploded volcanically. The eruption of Mount St. Helens sent a plume of ash miles into the atmosphere while devastating 200 square miles of forested landscape with molten magma and claiming fifty-seven lives.

It was a day that reminds us of the power of nature that points to the power of the Creator. It was also a day that reminds us of an all-too-important lesson. That ultra-fine silt-like Mount Saint Helens ash that blanketed our state for weeks, in time would become fertilizer for new growth that beautifies the base of the remaining mountain.

That same ash was used by skilled glassmakers to create treasured art that is breathtakingly beautiful. I have an ornate ornament that celebrates an easily forgotten maxim: out of crises and chaos come new opportunities and new beginnings where God calibrates His creation. In the words of the prophet Isaiah, *God gives us beauty for ashes, gladness for mourning and praise in the place of despair.* All for the display of God's splendor.

Lord, teach us to number our days. Help us to seize this day and make the most of it by learning from the past even as we trust You for what the future holds.

33

Something you may not know about me is that I play alto saxophone. I started in fifth grade and played through college. I've lost my embouchure through lack of practice so don't expect me to solo any time soon.

Being part of a symphonic wind ensemble was a meaningful experience. Gifted conductors chose challenging music that stretched our ability. As we perfected our parts, we experienced the rich beauty of harmonic music that touched the soul. If you were a serious musician in school and beyond, you know the unique joy that comes from making music in addition to listening to it.

As I listen to Lauren, our classical-musician daughter, practice and perform, I vicariously relive the joys I knew being part of an orchestra or band.

Even if you never played a musical instrument, you understand what it means to be part of an organization that is comprised of several sections. What your section does is distinct from others. And because it is unique, it is indispensable. The organization demands what you bring to the table.

That is a biblical principle as well. In his letters to young churches, the apostle Paul celebrated the importance of teamwork and body life. He compared the church to a human body in which each limb, organ and feature was complementary. We have something to offer and we need what others offer.

Back in the fifties Teresa Brewer released a record that climbed the charts. You likely remember it. It went like this:
Got along without you before I met you.
Gonna get along with you now.

Great lyrics don't necessarily translate into good theology. According to St. Paul, once we become connected to the family of God, we can't get along without each other. We need each other.

And that's what makes sheltering in place especially challenging and frustrating. We miss each other because we need each other. But gratefully we are finding creative ways to contribute our part to the larger whole. Just like those Zoom performances you are no doubt seeing on TV, our voice is added to other voices and the result is a virtual choir making a joyful noise.

34

For the past two decades I have been writing a weekly poetry blog. It's called *Rhymes and Reasons*. It's an opportunity to reflect in rhyme on current events, popular culture and faith. In all that time, I have never missed a week. Some weeks I struggle to find the idea I want to develop. And since my copy needs to be posted by late Thursday night, depending on issues related to my daytime job, there are some weeks when I barely meet my deadline.

Last week I was having one of those wrestling matches with myself. I didn't want to write yet another poem about COVID. But what? Then it dawned on me. Why not a verse celebrating the faithful work of first responders?

As the designated chaplain for the Mercer Island Police and Fire Departments, I see the tireless effort of EMTs and paramedics up close and personal. Because their red aid car visits our campus on a regular basis, our residents have just cause to celebrate the role paramedics play in our lives. Here's what I wrote:

The paramedics in my town
are not a pair. They're three.
In uniformed allegiance, they save lives.
There's no way the Lone Ranger
could accomplish what they do.
These masked men answer calls for hearts and hives.

They lift someone who's fallen down.
They rescue cats in trees.
They chauffeur broken hips to the ER.
These first-responder heroes
are deserving of our praise.
Like the wisemen, they find us where e'er we are.

Responsively they answer
when you dial 9-1-1.
In minutes they arrive. They waste no time.
Their mission is our welfare
and their motive is quite clear.
They want to help a loved one (yours or mine).

Evergreen Covenant Church here on Mercer Island is less than a hundred yards from the Mercer Island Fire Department. When I was pastor at Evergreen, I continued a tradition begun by our friend, Bud Palmberg, who was pastor at Evergreen for 26 years. Whenever a fire truck or aid car left the station house with their sirens blaring, I would stop mid-sentence and lead in prayer for those who were on their way to an emergency.

When you hear or see the aid car on your street, I would invite you to stop and pray for the one needing help, as well as those who are rushing to help that individual.

35

During the summer of 1969, I traveled in a high school church choir touring the east coast. We sang beneath the dome of U. S. Capitol rotunda as then Senator Henry "Scoop" Jackson looked on. In preparation for the tour, the director of the choir assigned me a speaking part. It was a narration he expected me to commit to memory. I did. More than fifty years later, I can still recite it:

America's greatness can only be equated with America's God. The average age of the world's greatest civilizations is about 200 years. During those 200 years, these nations progressed through the following sequence: From bondage to spiritual faith; from spiritual faith to great courage; from great courage to liberty; from liberty to abundance; from abundance to selfishness; from selfishness to complacency; from complacency to apathy; from apathy to dependence; and from dependence to bondage again.

And then I said, *In just a few short years our country will be two hundred years old.*

Years later I did some internet research and discovered that this quote is generally attributed to Sir Alexander Fraser Tytler. A contemporary of Thomas Jefferson, Tytler was a Scottish writer and historian who served as Professor of Universal History at the University of Edinburg.

His scenario is a haunting one. And whereas we recognize that God does not love America any more than any other nation on earth, God desires the worship and obedience of all peoples and that failure to honor God has consequences.

In the midst of the global pandemic, let's prayerfully reflect on the blessings we have enjoyed living in our country and acknowledge the hand of God that has accounted for so much we don't deserve. And let us thank God for the generous sacrifice of those who were willing to give their lives so that the liberties we too-often take for granted would not wither and die.

And let us remember the words from Scripture that declare, *Blessed is the nation whose God is the Lord.* (Psalm 33:12)

36

If I were to ask you what your most memorable Memorial Day was, how would you answer? Is there a particular holiday that would come to mind?

My most memorable Memorial Day was in May 1983. My wife and I were celebrating our first wedding anniversary. Wendy was five months pregnant and I was finishing my Master of Divinity degree at North Park Seminary in Chicago.

Because my wife's youngest brother was a student at nearby Wheaton College, we invited Lee to join us for a picnic in a suburban Chicago forest preserve. I kid you not. It was one of the coldest days of the whole year. At least it felt that way.

What was it Mark Twain once said, *One of the coldest winters I ever spent was the summer I spent in San Francisco?* Well, it was kind of like that.

We did our best to enjoy roasting hotdogs over a portable barbecue grill. But we were miserable and could hardly wait to get back to our respective apartments.

Upon returning to the North Park campus, I received word that a call had come from Idaho. My beloved grandmother had just died earlier in the day. I thought back to the last time I had seen her. It was a few months after Wendy and I were married. While driving from Seattle to Chicago, we had stopped in Lewiston so I could see my grandma and preach at her church. It had been a very special visit. My dad's mom gave her seal of approval on my choice of a life partner. She affirmed me in my call to ministry. I had no idea I'd never see her again.

So, now every Memorial Day as I visit a nearby cemetery and recall heroes who have left their mark in our lives, I think back on that bittersweet Memorial Day and thank God for a godly woman who regularly prayed for me.

She is the same woman who prayed both her sons home from World War 2. My dad and his brother were Marines in the South Pacific. Dad never tired of telling my brother and me how his mom fervently prayed Psalm 91 as she knelt at her bed each night.

Whoever dwells in the shelter of the Most High
*   will rest in the shadow of the Almighty.*[a]
2 I will say of the LORD, "He is my refuge and my fortress,
*   my God, in whom I trust."*
3 Surely he will save you
*   from the fowler's snare*
*   and from the deadly pestilence.*
4 He will cover you with his feathers,
*   and under his wings you will find refuge;*
*   his faithfulness will be your shield and rampart.*
5 You will not fear the terror of night,
*   nor the arrow that flies by day,*
6 nor the pestilence that stalks in the darkness,
*   nor the plague that destroys at midday.*
7 A thousand may fall at your side,
*   ten thousand at your right hand,*
*   but it will not come near you. (Psalm 91:1-7)*

37

Our married daughter and her family came for dinner last night. And whereas Wendy's marinated flank steak on the grill was "to die for," the highlight of the evening was our 13-month-old granddaughter taking her first steps. I have proof on my wife's iPhone.

And what made it all the more exciting is that Ivy Joy was walking to me. That precious milestone of first steps caused me to reflect on my relationship with God. Ivy Joy's tumbles and falls in the process of taking steps were overshadowed by her effort to draw near to me. My Heavenly Father isn't at all that concerned with the number of times I fall if I am attempting to step out in faith and move toward Him.

I love the way the Lord likens his relationship to Israel as a caring parent:

It was I who taught Ephraim to walk,
*   taking them by the arms;*
but they did not realize
*   it was I who healed them.*
4 I led them with cords of human kindness,
*   with ties of love.*
To them I was like one who lifts
*   a little child to the cheek,*
*   and I bent down to feed them.* (Hosea 11:3-4)

Taking first steps is a great metaphor for moving toward maturity. My friends in Alcoholics Anonymous are quite public about the importance of taking steps toward personal growth. They celebrate the goal of walking forward in an awareness of a Higher Power and facing the challenges of life "one day at a time." Those in AA know that you have to take first steps first and then take the twelve steps in order.

Every day we have a chance to move ahead. To step out and explore new opportunities. We may not have a clear understanding of where our steps are leading us or what a new norm will look like. But that's okay. Our job is to make forward progress … in a direction that is God-honoring … and other-centered.

38

As I shared yesterday, our lives are defined by steps. First steps. Baby steps. Stumbles and falls give way to grown-up steps. One day, quite possibly, that little 13-month-old granddaughter will take her father's arm and walk a center aisle of a church to promise a lifetime of love to the love of her life.

But let's not forget about the importance of those who cheer us on as we learn how to walk. When my granddaughter took her first steps toward me, Ivy's parents, her sister, her aunt and her Nana could all be heard in the background. They were verbalizing their belief in little Ivy. They believed she could do it. And when she did, their affirmation could not be contained.

We all need cheerleaders as we take steps into new seasons and new challenges in our lives. As we face the lingering consequences of this coronavirus, we need each other. Some are making peace with giving up their car keys, swallowing hard as they realize that walking is now the new norm.

Others are learning to take baby steps, learning how to use a walker following a debilitating surgery or a stroke. Still others find themselves walking into a new world without the love of their life, having been separated by death or dementia or an unwanted divorce.

Others, like my friend Owen Hall, are discovering the delight of walking with God for the first time in the winter season of their lives. When Owen was eighty-five, a retired pastor's wife on our campus shared the Four Spiritual Laws with this gifted watercolor artist and led him into assurance of God's love. And Donna and her husband continued to cheer Owen on in his newfound faith in the months that followed.

In all these scenarios, we need cheerleaders. We need those encouraging us to keep at it. We need community. The one who penned the Epistle to the Hebrews knew the importance of having others in our corner verbalizing their praise:

And let us consider how to stir up one another to love and good works, not neglecting to meet together, as is the habit of some, but encouraging one another, and all the more as you see the Day drawing near. (Hebrews 10:24-25)

Whether it's a baby learning how to walk or a newlywed couple learning how to live out their vows, success is more likely when there are others on the sidelines modeling what it takes and voicing their approval.

39

This morning I'm feeling sad. I just received an email from the person who oversees the ministry of us Covenant Living chaplains. One of our colleagues, who just retired in his mid-sixties last year, is battling pancreatic cancer. The note indicated that Rocky had just entered hospice care.

I always viewed Rocky a rock star when we were in seminary. He had a part-time job working his way through school. He was a custodian at the campus bookstore. And one of his jobs was cleaning the bathrooms.

I was always impressed with his willingness to serve other people. It reminded me of what Jesus would do. Rocky was not too important to stoop to do the lowliest of work.

As I saw his name on the email about his declining health, I thought back to the fall of 1982 when I saw his initials on the back of the bookstore bathroom door where he had signed off on having completed a job that "someone had to do."

Hospice is a haunting word. It reminds us that someone is terminal. That they are going to die. But guess what? In a very real sense, we all are on hospice. Why? Because life is a terminal disease.

I have a signature expression that I repeat at every celebration of life. As we gather to remember people we have grown to love, I say, *Every memorial service we attend is one closer to our own.*

It's true! Every day is a gift. We can't take tomorrow for granted. And every day is a chance to follow our Lord's lead in finding ways to make a positive difference in the lives of the people around us. Let's not waste today. Let's embrace it with gratitude and humility. And let's look for ways to serve others. That's what Jesus did!

For the Son of Man did not come to be served but to serve and to give his life as a ransom for many. (Mark 10:45)

40

Disneyland prides itself as being the *happiest place on earth*. During COVID things weren't all that happy in Disneyland. It was closed up tighter than a drum for months.

We all need a happy place to which we can go when we are feeling bored, anxious, depressed, stressed out or afraid. Sometimes those happy places are actual and sometimes those places are virtual.

So, what are those virtual happy places in our lives? Places like our family photo albums that recall joyful times and fun places to which we've journeyed with people we love. Happy places include walks we take all alone down memory lane.

Happy memories are a great place to hole up when we are feeling down. Our happy place may be a corner of our living room where we feel cozy and warm as the sunshine pours through the window and drenches our favorite chair (in which we are seated) with light.

Our happy place may be a forested trail or a lakeside path. Walking that paved path and drinking in views of the water and the flowering bushes and the blossoming trees does more than a body good. It's good for our souls, too.

Finding that happy place that makes regular deposits of joy in the savings account of our heart is especially important during times of uncertainty. Wearing a mask and keeping physical distance is necessary and good. But they can't keep us entirely healthy. We need a dose of daily joy as well.

I love that verse in Proverbs that goes like this: *A merry heart does good like medicine.* (Proverbs 17:22) In other words, happiness is therapeutic. Joy (like a daily apple) will keep the doctor away. And did you know that an hour of hearty laughter will burn a hundred calories?

Let's hear it for laughter. Let's hear it for happiness. Let's hear it for a God who inspired a little known prophet to write, *The joy of the Lord is our strength.* (Nehemiah 8:10)

41

Have you ever heard of four-square living? It was first introduced by William Danforth, the founder of the Ralston Purina Company and Chex cereals.

Danforth's checkerboard-square logo on his company's products represented the four ways that Jesus grew and developed as recorded in Luke 2. Jesus grew in wisdom and in stature. He grew in favor with God and in favor with others.

Today I'd like us to consider *wisdom*. And I don't just mean book learning.

I think you would agree with me that intellectual curiosity cultivates a desire to live and irrigates a life God blesses. I work in a setting where 90th birthday parties are not that big a deal, but mind-stretching opportunities are.

I am impressed by those who are actively involved in book clubs and are engaged in discussions about movies or plays they've seen recently. The enthusiastic response to an interactive current-events program is impressive. The questions the presenter proposes are proof positive that the minds of our residents are definitely not on cruise control.

A few years ago more than 100 of our residents read through the entire Bible in a year. We called the adventure, "A Journey on Route 66." The questions and comments individuals contributed while traveling through all 66 books of holy writ were of the caliber to keep me on my toes as a chaplain. Healthy oldsters keep learning. Mind stretching engagement is a sign of healthy growth. It is a necessity for a balanced lifestyle.

Speaking of reading through the entire Bible, when you read through the Old Testament you realize how certain individuals lived longer than we do today. And those older people didn't coast. They kept on going, connected to their families and to their God. They remained useful. And a key contributor to remaining useful is remaining mentally engaged.

Wisdom is more than reading and learning. Wisdom implies applying what we read and learn. There's a difference between knowing facts and being wise. Smart alecks tend to be wise guys but are neither smart nor wise.

Wise ones are those who seek to learn from what they know to be true having grasped the truth from what they've experienced through exposure.

It was Jesus who said, *Let him who has ears to hear, hear.* In other words, hearing does not automatically mean listening. It requires reflection. It requires action.

In this complicated season of a paralyzing pandemic and protesting injustice, we would do well to reflect on facts and listen to one another. Or as Jesus suggested, *Let him who has ears to hear, hear.* (Matthew 11:15)

42

Do you not know that your bodies are temples of the Holy Spirit, who is in you, whom you have received from God? You are not your own. (1 Corinthians 6:19)

As I mentioned previously, William Danforth's four-square living philosophy of life was based on what he read in the second chapter of Luke: *Jesus grew in wisdom and stature and in favor with God and man.* (Luke 2:52)

I don't think I'll ever eat a bowl of Rice Chex again without seeing the checkerboard-square logo in the corner of the cereal box and thinking of Mr. Danforth. And Rice Chex is a gluten-free breakfast option that is a healthy choice for those concerned with their physical wellbeing.

Eating healthy is definitely an obvious way to focus on our physical development. Fresh fruits, vegetables, lean meats. Getting our protein, limiting our saturated fat intake. The dining staff on our campus does a great job helping us eat right. I give God thanks for our entire dining team at Covenant Living at the Shores.

Physical exercise mitigates against the consequences of aging. Stretching one's mind isn't enough to maintain a balanced life. Physical stretching and balance exercises are also important. So, too, are the "sit and get fit" workouts with our fitness director.

Scripture teaches that our bodies are the temple of the Holy Spirit. Such sacred edifices deserve upkeep and refurbishment. I am impressed with the disciplined regimen that our Covenant Living campuses promote that find our residents across the country on treadmills, clocking miles on exercise bikes or walking laps. Kudos to our President, Terri Cunliffe, for her vision that embraces our wellbeing.

Wellness celebrates health and physical health is essential to living the life God blesses. When we take care of our bodies, we sleep better at night and we are less apt to get sick. Physical wellness impacts our emotional health as well. And in these days when we are emotionally impacted by current events, we need to take preventative precaution by taking care of the machines God gave us.

All that to say, be careful how much news you watch. Even more, be careful how much TV you watch. Know when to turn it on and when to turn it off. Get your steps in each day.

Get your 40 winks. Don't skimp on sleep. Make friends with your pillow. And if you have restless nights, don't hesitate to nap when needed.

Walk the halls. Walk the lake path. Walk to the Lodge. And don't forget your weights. Wait to snack. Wait before you worry. Wait before you retaliate. But don't wait to pray. In fact, let's do that right now.

43

As we've discovered, the founder of the Ralston Purina Company developed his company logo and his life philosophy from the Gospels. *Jesus grew in wisdom and stature and in favor with God and with man.* (Luke 2:52) Those four areas comprise a balanced life that pave the way to shalom and aloha.

So what about "experiencing favor with God?" The spiritual dimension of our lives is often the most overlooked one. It was St. Augustine who said a very long time ago, *Thou hast made us for Thyself O God and our hearts are restless until they rest in Thee.*

It was a 17th century philosopher by the name of Blaise Pascal who said every human being has a God-shaped hole that only God can fill.

In other words, we are spiritual beings even if we are not overtly religious. We have a spiritual dimension because we were created in the image of our Creator. Spiritual expression expands the windshield of one's worldview. The essence of a healthy balanced life is rooted in the soil of the soul. When we are not forced to worship virtually, our residents attend twenty different congregations in Greater Seattle. Why? Well the answer is fairly simple. Faith is foundational to a meaningful life (and death).

I've watched countless residents conclude their earthly journey without fear or regrets. A personal relationship with their Creator equates to an assurance of eternal life. And when it comes to the end of life, the bottom line is our relationship with the living God.

So, how does one explore the spiritual dimension of their life? The most obvious answer is prayer. If you were to boil down prayer to its most basic definition, it would be "practicing the presence of God." Prayer is acknowledging God in the midst of your life, your concerns, your questions, your doubts, your fears, your hopes, your gratitude and your regrets.

Prayer is not just saying words to God. It's recognizing that God is aware of what captivates our attention. Prayer is being mindful of One who is capable of reading our minds and redeeming our hearts.

44

As you know by now, the four dimensions of four-square living was what William Danforth used as his rule for life. It also accounted for the recognizable logo on his Ralston-Purina products (including Chex cereals). Be honest, now. Did you really know that the checkerboard-square logo was derived from Luke 2:52 where it says *Jesus grew in wisdom and stature and in favor with God and in favor with man?*

The life God blesses is a life that is balanced in these four areas: intellectual, physical, spiritual and social. Those components comprise wholeness. Wellness is a term we hear a lot of these days. Wellness is the result of harmony, peace and balance. A synonym for wellness is aloha. And a life clothed in aloha is more than simply wearing a Hawaiian shirt.

That aloha wellness (or shalom balanced life) includes a life of relating to those around us. The life God blesses requires social interaction because He created us to be social beings. Relational involvement reduces the alienation of loneliness. Statistics indicate that people who conclude their lives in a retirement community live some ten years longer than those who live alone. In Genesis we read, *It is not good for man to live alone!*

The rest of the Bible illustrates the importance of community. I've witnessed that first hand, and so have you.

That's why this season of social distancing is very difficult. It's counterintuitive. It's counter to how we were created. We were made for community. And that's why (even against the backdrop of a pandemic) we must find creative ways to interact with each other. Four-square living means taking our cues from the One who was the epitome of wellness.

Here's a little rhyme I wrote that celebrates what I believe to be true about the aloha life of wellness:

I have come to see that wellness
is much more than being fit.
A healthy body needs a healthy soul.
And while dieting and exercise
can do a body good,
a person really needs a higher goal.

It's great to run a marathon
or jog five times a week,
but running after peace has merit, too.
And while walking before supper
can burn dreaded calories,
a daily walk with God is good for you.

To bend and flex has merit.
So, we strive to stay in shape.
As we age we must maintain agility.
But God also wants to stretch us
to expand our usefulness.
It's His will that we become all we can be.

Yes, our bodies are a temple
that deserve refurbishment
lest (through disrepair) they start to fall apart.
But a temple's just a building
if it's just an empty shell.
So let's exercise our souls and guard our hearts.

45

It's a great day to choose to turn off the news and make some news of your own. In other words, today is a great day to choose to embrace something you really love doing and dance with that throughout the day.

What brings you joy? What causes your eyes to light up and go tilt? What stirs your cocoa? What floats your boat? What do you just love to do? In other words what keeps you stayin' alive? Painting, poetry, knitting, carving, sculpting, hiking, writing, reading?

When I was a divinity school student at Fuller Seminary, three days a week I drove with a couple of my roommates to the local YMCA for a fitness class. On the way we listened to the radio. One song I remember that was getting a lot of airtime back then was the Bee Gees song *Staying Alive*. It's part of the soundtrack from the movie *Saturday Night Fever*.

Some of you probably remember the lyrics:

Got the wings of heaven on my shoes
I'm a dancin' man and I just can't lose
You know it's alright, it's okay
I'll live to see another day
Whether you're a brother
or whether you're a mother
You're stayin' alive, stayin' alive
Feel the city breakin' and everybody shakin'
And we're stayin' alive, stayin' alive

Ah, ha, ha, ha, stayin' alive, stayin' alive

I loved the music from that movie. There is another movie I love that wasn't known for its soundtrack. It was known for its poignant dialogue. Given my love for poetry, it probably doesn't surprise you that I'm referring to *Dead Poet's Society*.

In a memorable scene Mr. Keating, the teacher portrayed by Robin Williams, gathers his students around and says:

We read and write poetry because we're members of the human race, and the human race is filled with passion. And business, law, medicine, and engineering are noble pursuits and necessary to sustain life. But poetry, beauty, romance, love — these are what we stay alive for.

I love that line. In this season of pandemic when the medical professionals and frontline healthcare workers are working overtime to keep us staying alive, what are we staying alive to do? Great question?

We weren't meant to just exist. We weren't created to while away the remaining time God grants us on this earth doing diddly squat.

Jesus left no doubt about the reason he came into this world. He wanted us to do much more than just stay alive. His purpose was that we experience all the abundance life has to offer. He said, *I have come that you might have life and live it to the full.* (John 10:10)

I like the way that sounds. I like that kind of God. A kind God with joyful intentions. God wants us to seize the day and waltz with what brings us unending joy. Have I made myself *abundantly* clear?

46

What do you do for recreation? Walk? Bike? My friend John Sager likes to fly model airplanes. Dave Wellman, Dave Selvig, Pete Baird and Janet Robinson like to golf. Our friends John and Kathy Willson like to garden. Maybe you're like Nancy Axell, Dee Tucker and Donna Palmberg. Maybe you like to create watercolor masterpieces. Someone I know rather well likes to write poetry. But maybe you find enjoyment in a daily crossword puzzle or a jigsaw puzzle. Do you enjoy baking?

Here's your invitation to identify what you love doing and then dance with that throughout the day. Recreation restores, renews, relaxes and recalibrates. It's a way to start over.

The root word for recreation is "re-create." Did you know there's a wonderful Christian hymn that talks about God re-creating? It's one of my favorites. It was written by Eleanor Farjeon in East Sussex, England back in 1931. She was given the task as a children's author of writing a poem for young people that would celebrate the gifts of each day.

The poet's words were put to a familiar Scottish tune. It was quite singable but didn't gain in popularity for 40 years. In 1971 a contemporary British folk singer by the name of Cat Stevens released it on one of his albums. The hymn I'm referring to is *Morning Has Broken*.

The lyrics paint a picture of the Garden of Eden and the freshness and newness of an unblemished world. It's in this place we find

God enjoying his favorite form of recreation. God takes each day and re-creates His world.

That's what is so beautiful about the gift of each new day. It's a chance to begin again. To start over. To establish new ways of thinking about life and relating to others.

Morning has broken like the first morning
Blackbird has spoken like the first bird
Praise for the singing
Praise for the morning
Praise for them springing fresh from the Word.

Sweet the rain's new fall, sunlit from heaven
Like the first dew fall on the first grass,
Praise for the sweetness of the wet garden,
Sprung in completeness where His feet pass.

Mine is the sunlight,
Mine is the morning
Born of the One Light Eden saw play.
Praise with elation, praise every morning,
God's recreation of the new day.

47

Speaking of *Morning Has Broken*, that hymn came to mind earlier this week as I witnessed a gorgeous sunrise very early in the morning from one of my favorite lookouts. As often happens when I find myself in a breathtaking place, I start to write.

Words flowed from my heart as I reflected on the contrast between the beauty of the sky and ugliness in our world that is being documented by daily headlines. There is so much that isn't right. So much pain. So much fear. Cities are beginning to unlock the lockdown but normal has a new definition. I thought about the evil in our world as well as the sinful nature that punctuates our fallen humanity.

Here's what I typed on my iPhone:

While morning has broken,
our world's in a mess.
The virus still threatens
and causes us stress.
But even more deadly
is what lurks within.
It, too, is a virus.
God's Word calls it sin.

Sin masks racist motives.
It keeps us apart.
Sin spreads just like COVID
as hate fills our hearts.

But love is a vaccine.
That's where hope begins.
Love dares to say "sorry"
again and again.

Love mends what is broken.
It breaks what needs fixed.
Love brings us together
without stones and sticks.
It risks being slighted.
It owns ugly pride.
It claims God's forgiveness
for which Jesus died.

Yes, love is the key. And love is possible. It's a choice. It's a daily choice. With the dawn of every morning, we have the chance to choose love over fear. Love over hate. Others over self.

Speaking of daily choices, every sunrise is a reminder that we have a chance to start anew each day. The words of Jeremiah convey that thought. In his journal that we call *Lamentations* we read, *The steadfast love of the Lord never ceases. His mercies never come to an end. They are new every morning.* (Lamentations 3:22)

Why don't we take our cues from our Creator? And live a life of love one day at a time?

48

In the fall of 1970 I began attending a school that would shape my life in profound ways. The very first week was memorable. That was the week I encountered the woman I would one day marry. My final week at Seattle Pacific University four years later was also most memorable.

As I crossed the stage to receive my degree at commencement, the Academic Dean was so nervous about pronouncing my last name correctly, he messed up my first name. Instead of calling me GREG, he called me GEORGE.

I don't know about you, but I have a lot of Georges in my life. There's George Toles and George Duff and George Minerva and George Warren and George Eaton and George Johnson and George Elia and George Munzing. And as a devoted fan of the movie "It's a Wonderful Life," I certainly can't forget old mossback George Bailey! Hee Haw!

But a new George came into my life this past year. He entered your life, too. What's his name? George Floyd! That's right.

When George Floyd was eight years old, the young black boy wrote an essay in second grade describing what he wanted to do when he grew up. Because Thurgood Marshall, an African American, was an esteemed Supreme Court Justice, that's what young George wanted to be. He wanted his life to count. He wanted to make a difference.

Even as a kid, justice was on his mind. Maybe you saw George's second-grade teacher hold up that homework before the news cameras. Waynel Sexton was so impressed with what he wrote, she kept it all these years.

Well, George got his wish. Albeit tragically, his life has impacted our nation in a big way. With his dying breath, he oxygenated the civil rights movement and resuscitated Mother Liberty's call for justice.

There's a verse that became important to me while at Seattle Pacific. It's found in Mark 10:45: *For the Son of man did not come to be served but to serve and to give his life as a ransom for many.*

I'm not equating the sacrifice of an imperfect human being with the redemptive death of the sinless son of God. But I am observing that our service of humanity historically has been irrigated with the blood of those who died on the frontlines of freedom.

49

Children of the Heavenly Father is a favorite hymn of those of a Scandinavian background who grew up going to a Covenant Church or a Lutheran Church. It was written by Lina Sandell. Lina was the daughter of a Lutheran pastor in Smolland, Sweden.

From what I've read, Lina greatly loved and admired her father. As a child she was quite frail and sickly. She preferred to be with him in his study rather than play with other kids outdoors.

At an early age she had been stricken with a partial paralysis that confined her to bed much of the time. Though the physicians considered her chance for a complete recovery hopeless, her parents always believed that God would in time make her well again.

When she was twelve, something happened that impacted her young life in a major way. One Sunday morning, while her parents were in church, Lina began reading the Bible and praying earnestly. When her parents returned, they were amazed to find her dressed and walking freely. After this experience of physical healing, Lina began to write verses expressing her gratitude and love for God. She published her first book of spiritual poetry when she was sixteen.

Ten years later when she was twenty-six, Lina accompanied her father on a boat ride across Lake Vattern. Tragically, her father fell overboard and drowned while Lina looked on in horror. Although Lina had written many hymn texts prior to this tragic experience, now more than ever, poetic thoughts began to flow from her broken heart. All of her hymns reflect a tender, childlike trust in her Savior and a deep sense of His abiding presence in her life.

Perhaps these familiar words will mean all the more to you now that you know "the rest of the story."

Children of the heav'nly Father
Safely in His bosom gather
Nestling bird nor star in Heaven
Such a refuge e'er was given

Neither life nor death shall ever
From the Lord, His children sever
Unto them His grace He showeth
And their sorrows all He knoweth

Though He giveth or He taketh
God His children ne'er forsaketh
His, the loving purpose solely
To preserve them, pure and holy

No matter how many candles will adorn your birthday cake this year, you, like Lina, are a child in need of a Heavenly Father's protection, comfort and care.

50

It's another Choose Day. So will you choose to add to your list of complaints and inconveniences related to the coronavirus? Or will you choose to list the many ways God has been faithful over the past several months?

Thomas Chisholm chose the latter. He focused on the faithful attributes of God picturing the Almighty as a father that is committed to provide for the needs of His family.

Thomas O. Chisholm was born in a log cabin in rural Kentucky in 1866. That was the year after Abraham Lincoln (another Kentuckian born in a log cabin) died. He became a public school teacher at the age of sixteen and an editor of his hometown newspaper at the age of twenty-one. Chisholm became a Christian at the age of twenty-seven and was eventually ordained as a pastor.

Ill health prevented him from continuing in the ministry, and he found his niche as an insurance salesman, which enabled him to provide for his family.

A prolific poet, Chisholm wrote a poem in 1923 celebrating God's faithfulness in his life thus far. He based his poem on Lamentations 3:22-23: *The steadfast love of the Lord never ceases, his mercies never come to an end; they are new every morning; great is your faithfulness.*

He sent his verse to a friend who was affiliated with both the Moody Bible Institute and Hope Publishing Company and his friend set the poem to music. In 1953, at a Billy Graham Crusade in

Great Britain, George Beverly Shea introduced Thomas Chisholm's hymn to the Christian world. It was immediately popular.

If you hadn't guessed by now, I'm referring to the well-known hymn *Great is Thy Faithfulness*. For those of you who don't know the lyrics, they go like this:

Great is thy faithfulness, O God my Father;
There is no shadow of turning with thee;
Thou changest not, thy compassions, they fail not;
As thou hast been, thou forever wilt be.

Not only does Chisholm refer to God as Father, in the second stanza he illustrates the power of a father's presence in a person's life. A father's active role in a child's life both cheers and guides.

Pardon for sin and a peace that endureth,
Thine own dear presence to cheer and to guide;
Strength for today and bright hope for tomorrow,
Blessings all mine with ten thousand beside!

And then there is that memorable refrain:

Great is thy faithfulness! Great is thy faithfulness!
Morning by morning new mercies I see;
All I have needed thy hand hath provided;
Great is thy faithfulness, Lord, unto me

51

I got to know Judge Jack Scholfield when I first became the chaplain at Covenant Living at the Shores. This Superior Court Judge in Washington State found faith in One who had conquered death near the end of his ninety-five years of life. Although a wooden gavel had symbolized his commitment to law and justice for most of his adult life, Jack died clutching a little wooden holding cross. Fingering a symbol of mercy and grace, my friend breathed his last.

When Jack's son, Jim, helped me plan the memorial service, he told me he wanted to make sure the celebration of life included the singing of a published hymn Jack's father had written. I was dumbfounded. I didn't know Jack (a nominal church-goer at best) had a religious upbringing.

When Jack's son told me the name of the hymn, I couldn't believe it. *Saved, Saved* was a gospel hymn I'd sung in my pastor-father's church growing up. I looked up the origin of the hymn on Google. Sure enough, it was written by Jack Scholfield, Sr. I learned that the judge's father had been the song leader for a turn-of-the-century evangelist by the name of Mordecai Ham. At a revival meeting in Gonzales, Texas in 1911, Scholfield witnessed a man in the crowd come forward at the conclusion of the sermon crying out, "I'm saved! I'm saved! I'm saved!"

Following the service, Jack's dad went to his hotel room and penned the words and music to a song he introduced the following night. Two decades later that same evangelist was preaching in

Charlotte, North Carolina when a tall lanky sixteen-year-old went forward to commit his life to Christ, echoing the words of Jack Scholfield's hymn. That young man was none other than Billy Graham.

During my short friendship with Judge Jack, I had no idea of his spiritual heritage. But following his death, I realized he had passed from this life to the next experiencing the truth of his father's lyrics: *Life now is sweet and my joy is complete for I'm saved, saved, saved!*

As we live through the uncertainty of a global pandemic, we find ourselves grasping straws as to how it will all end. May the words of Paul in Romans 8 reassure us that God has a way of working out a plan that can complete our joy even as He saves us from calamity:

All things work together for the good of those who are called according to God's purpose. (Romans 8:28)

52

Day by Day and With Each Passing Moment is one of my all-time favorite hymns. It's a folk hymn often sung to a guitar accompaniment. When I became part of The Evangelical Covenant Church as a young adult, I discovered its Scandinavian hymnody resonated with my Norwegian heritage.

Lina, often called the Fanny Crosby of Sweden, wrote the lyrics to this hymn after the tragic death of her father whom she dearly loved. The references to heartache and sorrow are bold and candid. But hers was a faith that embraced bane as well as blessing.

Her pastor-father had influenced her young faith in a profound way. And even though his death seemed senseless and premature, Lina refused to blame God.

Instead, she took to heart the fact that God orchestrates the details of our lives for our good and His glory. She understood what Paul celebrated in his letter to the Christians in Philippi: *My God will meet all your needs according to the riches of His glory in Christ Jesus.* (Philippians 4:19)

Lina's special relationship with her loving and compassionate father definitely shaped her view of God. It's obvious by the way she describes her Heavenly Father's provision and care.

Day by day and with each passing moment,
Strength I find to meet my trials here;
Trusting in my Father's wise bestowment,
I've no cause for worry or for fear.
He whose heart is kind beyond all measure
Gives unto each day what He deems best--
Lovingly, its part of pain and pleasure,
Mingling toil with peace and rest.

Ev'ry day the Lord Himself is near me
With a special mercy for each hour;
All my cares He fain would bear, and cheer me,
He whose name is Counselor and Pow'r.
The protection of His child and treasure
Is a charge that on Himself He laid;
"As thy days, thy strength shall be in measure,"
This the pledge to me He made.

Help me then in eve'ry tribulation
So to trust Thy promises, O Lord,
That I lose not faith's sweet consolation
Offered me within Thy holy Word.
Help me, Lord, when toil and trouble meeting,
E'er to take, as from a father's hand,
One by one, the days, the moments fleeting,
Till I reach the promised land.

What a beautiful picture of our Heavenly Father's care. Doesn't it make you want to reach out and take that extended hand? I invite you to walk with that loving One today.

53

A little gold statue by the name of Oscar is awarded each year to the best actors in Hollywood. Our family enjoys watching the Academy Awards. In fact, we make it an annual tradition. Back when our kids were small, we dressed up for the occasion. I wore a tux. My wife wore an evening dress and our girls wore something sparkly and flowing. We'd fill out our ballots and then score ourselves as the results were announced.

Isn't it funny that ours is a culture that honors people who make a living pretending. Actors are rewarded for spending their lives offering convincing performances of characters who are not real. Jesus had a real hard time with people who play-acted. They were called Pharisees. Jesus called them hypocrites. The Greek word for hypocrite meant "one who acts." It referred to stage actors in the first century who wore masks.

Unlike the face coverings we are called to wear, the actors' masks were not meant to keep them from getting a virus. The purpose was to cover up their countenance. A mask was the means by which they could mislead the audience.

What angered Jesus was the fact that the Pharisees' religious works were not sincere. Their supposed devotion was a pretense. They were pretenders. There was a not-so-obvious disconnect between what was on the inside and what was on the outside. The Pharisees were actors deserving of an Oscar. Jesus called them whitewashed tombs filled with dead men's bones.

What God desires is congruence in our lives. He desires that our behavior match our beliefs. Someone once said: *Imitation is the sincerest form of flattery.* Here's an even better quote: *A sincere Christ-follower is the one most worthy of imitating.*

As second-rate actors we just might be good enough to fool those around us into thinking we are more godly than we really are. But why should we try? God sees behind our masks. He knows what's in our hearts. We can't fool Him. God desires integrity.

With David let's pray, *Create in me pure heart, O God, and renew a steadfast spirit within me. Restore the joy of my salvation.* (Psalm 51:10)

54

In the old days, a clapboard was used by Hollywood filmmakers to mark a scene and "a take" so that they could be more easily identified during the editing process when sound was added to the visual performance.

You probably recall the three words as well as the sequence with which those three words were spoken by the director just before shooting a scene commenced:

Lights! Camera! Action!

We learned similar words as kids when competing in the 100-yard dash. *Ready! Set! Go!*

But Jesus also had three words for which he became known by his disciples. Do you remember what they were? *Ask. Seek. Knock.*

Since I'm a guy whose playmates are words, I can't help but find humor in things to which most people are oblivious.

I even told a friend of mine who is a cartoonist about a funny thought I had that might be worthy of a cartoon.

Can you picture Jesus on the side of the mountain multiplying the little boy's lunch of five loaves and two fish? He's wearing a face mask. The disciples are, too. And he says to the crowd of thousands who aren't wearing face coverings, *Mask and it shall be given unto thee.*

I know. It's a bit cheesy. Perhaps it borders on being a bit sacrilegious. But I can't help but think Jesus has a sense of humor. *Mask and it shall be given unto thee."*

We are called to ask, seek and knock. In other words, we are called to be persistent in our praying. To persevere in our petitions. To be intent in our intercessions.

Ours is a Heavenly Father who, like an earthly father, wants us to admit our needs and sincerely seek Him. When your children came to you with a heart-felt request, you were grateful that they trusted you to ask for what you alone could give.

Ask, seek, knock … those are the words the director of our lives speaks inviting us to play our part as children of the living God.

55

It's true. Hollywood does intersect our lives as believers. For review, there's the irony of how our culture makes celebrities out of those who make a living by pretending when Jesus put down the Pharisees for being play-actors. That's what the word hypocrite means.

Yesterday we considered God's version of *Lights! Camera! Action!* From the director's seat we hear a loving Father inviting us to come to Him with our requests when we've forgotten our lines or simply don't know what to do. *Ask! Seek! Knock!*

You see, at the corner of Hollywood and Vine there is more than meets the eye. The tangible symbols of tinsel town provide us with food for thought (when it comes to our faith). And I don't mean hot buttered popcorn or Junior Mints.

In our garage I keep a big format film canister from the good old days. I don't know where I got it, but we use it each year for our Oscar Night display. The canister is just a container. It really doesn't matter all that much. What counts is the film inside.

The same is true for us. We tend to get overly fixated on our outward appearance. We stress over our appearance. Wrinkles. Weight. Gray hair. We allow the bathroom mirror to dictate our mood. We give the bathroom scale way too much weight. (Grin!)

Who was it that said, *Physically fit people just die healthier?*

What matters most is not the container we will never be fully satisfied with. It's what's inside that counts. Our personality. Our motives. Our hopes, dreams and desires.

Our soul is the feature film that people are dying to see. It's what we are dying to project so others can enjoy the real us.

Let's not let Hollywood's fascination with outward beauty and popularity and pretense prevent us from focusing the camera on what the Director of our lives is most interested in. His script is worth memorizing.

What was it Jesus said? *25 Therefore I tell you, do not worry about your life, what you will eat or drink; or about your body, what you will wear. Is not life more than food, and the body more than clothes? 26 Look at the birds of the air; they do not sow or reap or store away in barns, and yet your heavenly Father feeds them. Are you not much more valuable than they? 27 Can any one of you by worrying add a single hour to your life?*

28 And why do you worry about clothes? See how the flowers of the field grow. They do not labor or spin. 29 Yet I tell you that not even Solomon in all his splendor was dressed like one of these. 30 If that is how God clothes the grass of the field, which is here today and tomorrow is thrown into the fire, will he not much more clothe you — you of little faith? 31 So do not worry, saying, 'What shall we eat?' or 'What shall we drink?' or 'What shall we wear?' 32 For the pagans run after all these things, and your heavenly Father knows that you need them.33 But seek first his kingdom and his righteousness, and all these things will be given to you as well. 34 Therefore do not worry about tomorrow, for tomorrow will worry about itself. Each day has enough trouble of its own. (Matthew 6:25-34)

56

Today is the first day of the rest of your life.

I had a poster hanging on my freshman dorm room at Seattle Pacific University fifty years ago with those words in big bold print. It reminded me of the importance of each day. I think that slogan is a helpful reminder to make the most of each day of our lives.

About twenty years ago I had the privilege of meeting news personality and commentator Paul Harvey at his broadcast studio in downtown Chicago. From the time I was a kid, I'd listened to Paul Harvey News and Comment on the radio as I got ready for school. So, sitting in on one of Paul Harvey's newscasts was a thrill for me.

I was asked to sit in the waiting room until Mr. Harvey was ready to meet me. On the wall was a framed Family Circus cartoon strip. It was a one-panel strip that showed sister explaining to brother that *Yesterday is the past. Tomorrow is the future. Today is a gift. That's why it's called the present.*

I had never seen that before. It resonated deeply. I love plays on words. In my Myers-Briggs code ENFP stands for Extravert, Intuitive, Feeling-oriented and Punster. (Well, actually the P stands for Perception, but Punster applies just the same).

Today IS a gift. That's why it's called the present. It's true. It's a package gift wrapped and delivered (not by Amazon) but by a

115

loving Creator who desires we rip up the wrapping paper and tear open the box and enjoy the miracle we call today.

It is a miracle. It's a 24-hour capsule of time never before experienced and never to be repeated. So let us not give in to the temptation of leaving this gift on the table or on the shelf to collect dust.

As if dangling by a spider's web,
our lives hang by a slender thread.
Our health is fragile
no matter how agile
or fit we think we may be.
And dreams shatter.
Plans change.
Death shows up unannounced.

So, we'd do well to ask the Lord to help us
pounce on each moment
and unwrap the present
and learn how to number our days
that we might gain a heart of wisdom
and live each day as a priceless gift from God.

What the psalmist wrote some three thousand years ago still applies: *This is the day the Lord has made. Let us rejoice and be glad in it.* (Psalm 118:24)

57

Today we'd do well to pray for our black-eyed relative who finds himself off balance and fighting to stand up for the principles that gave him life to begin with. So would you join me?

God, bless America.
Not because we deserve it.
Lord knows, we don't.
We have failed to live up to our potential.
We have denied equal rights
to those too-often wronged.
We have sacrificed godly principles
on the altar of personal privilege.
We have aborted life,
liberty and the pursuit of happiness
in exchange for power.
We have pledged allegiance to a flag
we too often have used to envelop our faith.

Amid "Black Lives Matter" signs
and "Make America Great Again" ballcaps,
we have lost sight of that
on which our founders initially focused …

A land of the free
and a home of the brave.
Out of many, one.
One nation under God,
with liberty and justice for all.

God, as dehumanizing relics of our past
are removed from courthouse circles
and city squares,
tear down the walls of hate
that continue to separate
all those created in Your image.
But, lest we be short-sighted
and impulsive prone,
give us courage to preserve
those monuments that call us to be
the best version of ourselves.
A goal for which we truly long.

Revive us as we attempt to repair
the foundations of freedom's ramparts
that have cracked and begun to crumble
through disregard of another's rights
and the disobedience of Your demands.

Lord, restore our vision for unity.
Rekindle our compassion for humanity.
Redeem decades of partisan divisions
that have bankrupted our trust in one another.
Renew our bruised and broken spirits
that we might dare to dream again.

Remind us of the words etched
on the base of Lady Liberty.
That we exist to welcome
those for whom the flame of freedom
has been extinguished …
The tired, the poor,
the huddled masses yearning to breathe free.

On this 244th anniversary
of our nation's birth,

as death has visited
more than 130,000 victims of COVID,
we humbly acknowledge
our need of You.
Gracious God, comfort the grieving
as only You can.
Contain the contagion.
Heal the suffering.
Enable those who are feverishly seeking a vaccine.
Guide those who are charged with leading us.

May those who live in the White House
(as well as those who live
in the house where we reside)
be aware of Your presence,
Your purpose
and our accountability to You
for goodness sake. Amen.

58

From Memorial Day through Labor Day, I wear one of my Hawaiian shirts to work. Over the years, it has become my fashion statement. Let me explain.

I love the spirit of Hawaii. It's the culture of aloha. If you've spent much time in the islands, you know what I'm referring to. The tropical paradise we call our fiftieth state exudes something special. People have time for one another. They don't take themselves too seriously. The music unique to Hawaii is tranquil and calming.

My friends Doug and Greg Tutmarc learned to play the Hawaiian steel guitar from their famous dad. I love to hear them play. It's relaxing and inspiring at the same time. As they play, I can picture the tropical breeze, I can see the swaying palm trees and I can hear the waves lapping on the sandy shore.

While the warm sunny weather of Hawaii is part of what makes the islands attractive, it's not just the weather. It's the aloha spirit that makes it so beautiful. Aloha means hello. It also means goodbye. But it means even more. Like the Hebrew word shalom, it has many meanings. Aloha conveys love and peace and wholeness.

So, by wearing Hawaiian shirts I want to picture God's aloha wherever I go. I want to take God's love and peace and wholeness into every room I enter. I want to suggest through my wardrobe that there is beauty in our world no matter how chaotic and vulnerable it may appear.

Truth be told, it doesn't take an aloha shirt to picture the beautiful world we long for. It just takes putting on Christ's countenance each day. Wearing a smile that suggests his kindness. Looking at another with understanding. Putting on patience as you would a piece of clothing. Yes, beauty begins with us.

For Mister Rogers, a beautiful day in his neighborhood began by donning a cardigan sweater and a pair of comfortable sneakers. For us, a beautiful day begins by clothing ourselves in the character of Christ. I love what it says in Isaiah 61:3 where we are called to *put on a garment of praise for the spirit of heaviness.*

That sounds like a great way to dress for the day, doesn't it?

59

Listen, do you want to know a secret? Well, actually it's not a secret. It was in the news. Ringo Starr, the drummer for *The Beatles,* recently celebrated his 80th birthday. That makes you feel old, doesn't it? It does me. I was eleven years old when the Fab Four invaded our nation and landed on *The Ed Sullivan Show.*

If you remember drummers by the name of Gene Krupa and Buddy Rich, you're also showing your age. One of my favorite drummers (who was coming into her own fifty years ago when I was about to start college) was Karen Carpenter. *We've Only Just Begun* was a favorite song as I was just beginning to figure out what I wanted to do with my life.

Another group that played the soundtrack of my college years was *The Association.* Do you remember their cherished hits? Songs like *Windy, Along Comes Mary* and *Never My Love.*

A few years ago I randomly met the drummer for *The Association* while in Wenatchee to visit my mom. Since then, Bruce Pictor has opened his life to me and we continue to email about matters of faith, friendship and music.

Drumming is a great metaphor for the cadence of Christianity. Lloyd Ogilvie, who was my pastor at Hollywood Presbyterian Church when I was in seminary, wrote a book called *The Drumbeat of Love.*

It illustrates how we as Christ followers provide the rhythm for the

Kingdom of God to advance in the world by the way we love each other. A good drummer lays down the basic track on which the rest of the band keeps time.

As you know, my daughter, Lauren, is a gifted flutist. She is part of a woodwind quintet that hopes to leave its mark in the music world. Their harmony is stunning. But due to COVID they have to create their music virtually. They can't play in the same room.

The key to their success is an electronic drum mechanism called a click track. It's an electronic metronome that allows each instrumentalist to play their part at the right time and keep time.

In times like these, the key to keeping in harmony and modeling the love of God for a confused and questioning world is providing a steady cadence of loving like Jesus. A constant rhythm of love, acceptance and forgiveness that doesn't skip a beat is what will attract others.

And even if you were not a percussionist in junior high band, you have what it takes to play drums. It's just a matter of being a steady source of kindness. I invite you to *Cherish* the thought and join me in being part of the association that asks "What would Jesus do?" And then do it!

In the same way, let your light shine before others, that they may see your good deeds and glorify your Father in heaven. (Matthew 5:16)

60

Today is a wonderful day. And the proof is in the living. Like the 1946 Frank Capra classic movie implies, ours is a wonderful life.

Speaking of *It's a Wonderful Life*, my good friend, Karolyn Grimes, who played George Bailey's little girl Zuzu, recently celebrated her 80th birthday. This multi-talented child actor was a Yankee Doodle baby born on the 4th of July in 1940. Sadly, her real off-screen life was anything but wonderful.

Although Karolyn Grimes was a very successful child actor who starred with such Hollywood greats as David Niven, Cary Grant and Jimmy Stewart, her wonderful life in tinsel town was cut short by having to grow up too soon. She lost both parents before she entered high school. She lost a marriage and then lost a teenage son to suicide. Gratefully, in the past thirty years, Karolyn has experienced wonderful dimensions of life denied her early on. And she gives God credit!

Have you ever thought about the word "wonderful"? It simply means "filled with wonder." Wonder-full. One of my favorite books of all times is called *A Touch of Wonder*. It's a book written by Arthur Gordon, who was a regular contributor to Reader's Digest.

When Wendy and I were dating, she gave me a copy of *A Touch of Wonder* for my birthday one year. Because Wendy knew I loved to write (and because her dad is a published author), she asked her dad to suggest a book that might be an appropriate gift for an author wanna-be.

A Touch of Wonder proved to be the perfect choice. In the short chapters of Gordon's book, the author opens the readers' eyes to the wonders there are to behold in each day if we have the eyes to see them.

Wonder is everywhere. But it takes expectation. You tend to see what you are looking for. And it takes time. It also takes a childlike curiosity and the observation skills of a child.

There's just something wonderful about children. They are full of wonder. Their wide-eyed excitement is contagious. But somewhere along the line we lose our sense of wonder. We quit looking for Godwinks.

Jesus talked about the importance of children. He said unless we become like little children we can't enter the Kingdom of God. No doubt he was referring to a child's candor, trust, believability and of course their wide-eyed wonder.

Today is a great day to ask the Lord to give us eyes that can see the Creator's fingerprints. May God give us a renewed sense of mystery in the little things of life. May God fill our tear ducts with drops that we can cry while witnessing a thing of beauty in this journey that really is a wonderful life.

Open my eyes that I may see wonderful things in your law. (Psalm 119:18)

61

Bastille Day in France marks the anniversary of storming the grand fortress in which political prisoners were held during the first moments of the French Revolution in 1789.

Just nine weeks after George Washington was sworn in as our nation's first president, the fortress was rattled and the fanfare of independence began to be trumpeted. But it would take another ten years for the revolution to run its course.

Today in France, Parisians are celebrating something that happened a long time ago. But they are also celebrating something much more current. There is joy in the city of lights over the reopening of the Eiffel Tower and the Louvre following COVID lockdowns. There is hopeful optimism that Notre Dame Cathedral will eventually rise from the ashes of the fire that nearly destroyed it a couple years back.

Today there is freedom in France from pervasive protocols put in place when the coronavirus first invaded Europe. Ironically, strict restrictions and quarantines paved the way to the freedom for which we Americans long.

It's also ironic that we Americans, who go all out celebrating Independence Day, are reaping the consequences of our independent strong-willed resistance to being told what to do. The images of coast-to-coast beach parties without masks or social distancing was shocking.

God's Word speaks to us about the importance of obeying authority figures in our lives, be they parents or government leaders. The Scriptures are replete with references to honoring God by keeping God's commands. But we are a strong-willed lot, we humans. We don't like to be told what to do no matter who's doing the telling. We resist authority. In the Old Testament the prophet Isaiah sees right through us.

He writes, *All we like sheep have gone astray. We have each turned to our own way.* (Isaiah 53:6).

Quite frankly, that's why we need a Savior. That's how we make sense of the principle of sacrifice in both the Old and New Testaments. Only by acknowledging how our self-centered mindset imprisons our soul can we acknowledge our desire to be set free.

And as Jesus is recorded as having said, *He whom the Son sets free is free indeed.* (John 8:36).

62

When is the last time you saw a photograph of yourself as a little baby? Recently, I was the unofficial photographer at my nephew's wedding in Fredericksburg, Virginia. The outdoor affair was beautifully choreographed against the backdrop of a finely manicured garden. But due to COVID, guests were few in number and socially distanced wearing masks.

It was a day to remember. It was especially meaningful for me because I had also been the photographer at Marshall's infant baptism at an Episcopal church in Charlottesville twenty-four years earlier.

Before the wedding day ended, I insisted on taking a photo of the groom with his mother (my sister-in-law). I wanted that pose because I recently had come across a baptism photo of Marshall with his mother.

Comparing the two photos, it was just as I had suspected. You can see in Marshall's face as an infant the very characteristics that define his young adult countenance.

Isn't it amazing? The uniqueness of our facial qualities is visible from the time we are born. But there is so much of life we've lived from the time we were born.

In the case of my nephew, the maturity I've witnessed in his life physically, emotionally and spiritually from one holy occasion to the most recent one is noteworthy. I thank God for the myriad of ways in which Marshall has grown. He is a testament of God's grace.

And so are you! As you look in the bathroom mirror tonight before you go to bed, take a good close look. Look beyond the wrinkles and the age spots to see the you that someone looking at your baby picture could still identify.

As you gaze at your reflection, thank the Lord for the way He has guided you and protected you and provided for you in the ups and downs of your journey. Ask God to continue to honor the promises many of your parents made on your behalf when you were presented for your Heavenly Father in baptism or dedication.

And while you're at it, thank the Lord that you are you. Celebrate the fact that you are indeed one of a kind.

I praise You for I am fearfully and wonderfully made. (Psalm 139:14)

63

I love to write. I've been writing a newspaper column most of my life. I wrote for my junior high school paper (*The Bear Facts*). I wrote for my high school paper (*The Apple Leaf*). And I wrote for my college newspaper (*The Falcon*). After moving to suburban Chicago, I started writing a weekly column for the *Daily Herald*.

I'm guessing some of you wrote for your school newspapers. Others of you likely wrote for a business journal or some professional publication. But even if you've never seen your name in the byline of a publication, you are a writer. Your words, actions and reactions, your countenance and your body language are being read by those who witness your life.

In 2 Corinthians 3, St. Paul agrees with me. To his friends who comprise the congregation in Corinth, he writes:

You yourselves are our letter, written on our hearts, known and read by everyone.

In other words, our words and actions are like a living letter. People can read us like a book. We are writers whether we realize it or not.

So, what then will be your life story?
It's a book that you're writing each day.
You're unique, so I guess it's a novel.
Still, your future's a big mystery.

Your story is bound to be noticed
by those who observe what you write.
Will your words offer Christ-like compassion
with phrases of reasoned insight?

Will your sentences question the culture
as you challenge the lies it conveys?
Will your paragraphs stand out in bold print
as you stand up to ungodly ways?

Will your story be read by the masses?
Or will it be left on some shelf?
The things that you write on each day's empty page
will result in a book called "Yourself."

64

Not long ago, the organization for which I work went through a rebranding. Covenant Retirement Communities changed their name to Covenant Living Communities and Services. Apparently, "retirement" is not a popular word or concept among us Baby Boomers. When we leave fulltime employment, we are inclined to redirect our energies and remain meaningfully engaged in life.

Each of the twelve campuses in our organization changed their name as well in order to fit within the new branding identity. Our campus in suburban Seattle went from Covenant Shores to Covenant Living at the Shores.

I've lost count of how many times I've goofed and referred to our campus by our old name. For our neighbors here on Mercer Island, I'm guessing it will always be Covenant Shores. Forty years of history is a lot to undo.

Name changes are Scriptural. The Old and New Testaments are replete with them. Abram became Abraham. Jacob became Israel. Simon became Peter. And Saul became Paul.

And speaking of Paul, the apostle of grace makes a case for each of us claiming a new name "Christian" which literally means "little Christ." He insists that as Christians we have a new identity.

Therefore, if anyone is in Christ, he is a new creation. The old has passed away; behold, the new has come. (2 Corinthians 5:17)

When our campus participated in the national rebranding initiative, I wrote a poem to help us celebrate our name change. It went like this:

It's a season of transitions.
There's still more we'd like to do.
There are options all around us.
Life is far from being through.
While it's true we make transitions,
God's promises abound.
And because the future beckons,
where we are is holy ground.

Covenant Living! Live with promise!
Covenant Living! Joy awaits!
With a staff inspired to serve us,
we have much to celebrate.

The gift of years is ours to open.
There is wonder to behold.
Growing older comes with blessings.
We are seasoned. We're not old.

There is promise in tomorrow.
Hope is found with each new day.
Covenant Living is our future
off'ring us a better way.

Covenant Living! Live with promise!
Covenant Living at "The Shores."
With a staff inspired to serve us,
we look ahead to so much more.

65

You no doubt can remember where you were when Neil Armstrong set foot on the moon. The date was July 20, 1969. I remember taking a photo of the moon with my Polaroid instant camera. No zoom lens. No fancy features. I had to draw an arrow on the print to show where the moon was.

A famous Chinese proverb says, *A journey of a thousand miles begins with one single step.* In other words, let's not minimize small steps that find us making major progress.

I have a relative who is a recovering alcoholic. She reminds me that those in Alcoholics Anonymous celebrate the importance of working the twelve steps a step at a time and a day at a time.

Goals that are worth pursuing are worth tackling in bite-size increments. Too often we give up because we don't acknowledge small steps.

Personal plans to exercise more begin with small increases in steps, weights or time spent working out. Personal plans to lose weight begin with small adjustments to calorie intake and calorie-burning activity.

Early in life we learned how dimes and dollars add up by regular deposits in a piggy bank. The desire to memorize passages of Scripture or much-loved verses of poetry can seem daunting until you reduce the task to bite-size chunks. Who was it who said, *Inch by inch anything's a cinch?*

The Lord's Prayer is a prayer we know by heart. In a way, that's a good thing. But the flip side of familiarity is that we sometimes say words without thinking about their meaning.

A key aspect of the Lord's Prayer is the line *Give us this day our daily bread.* In other words, we are asking our Heavenly Father to provide us with just what we need for today. There is much to be made of that request. In the little, there is a lot.

Daily bread isn't a week's worth of groceries. It doesn't equate to a month's supply of food in the freezer or non perishables in the pantry. Daily bread is daily bread. It's a reminder that we need to look to the Lord on a regular basis as we are taking each day a day at a time.

Small steps eventually take us a good long way.
A meaningful future begins by making the most of today.

66

Remember this childhood finger-play?

Here is the church. And here is the steeple.
Open the door and see all the people.

I thought about that nursery rhyme the other day. In light of COVID, when you open the door of most churches, you don't see many people.

Given what we are living through (and dying from), I decided the childhood verse needed to be revised. So I came up with a coronavirus version.

Here is the church. And here is the steeple.
Open the door and where are the people?

They're watching on desktops, on laptops and phones.
They're socially distanced. But they're not alone!

They're part of a Body that FaceTimes and Zooms.
They're one in the Spirit in various rooms.

The church ain't a building. It can't be shut down.
It's where you and I go, both home and downtown.

No! COVID can't kill us. When push comes to shove,
we thrive in the hard times, connected by love!

It's true. The church is not a building. The church is people. We are the church wherever we go. The Apostle Paul likens us to a human body. We are an organism. We're not static. We're dynamic.

And hard times and hardships don't douse us. If anything, they rouse us. When our backs are up against the wall, we find creative ways to find cracks and connect.

I miss worshiping in the same place and being able to see people's faces up close and personal. But with church services online a click away, people are experiencing church in winsome and wonderful ways even though we are physically distanced from one another.

Isn't that great? The coronavirus may be able to kill people, but it cannot kill the body of Christ.

I will build my church, and the gates of Hades will not overcome it.
(Matthew 16:18)

67

You're never fully dressed without a smile. Remember that line from a song in the Broadway musical *Annie?* It's true, isn't it? A smile completes your outfit.

I'd always heard that it takes fewer muscles to smile than it does to frown, but I did some fact checking the other day and discovered that's not really the case. It's not exactly fake news, but it's not entirely accurate. You use twelve muscles to smile and eleven muscles to frown.

Nonetheless, a smile is a whole lot more worthwhile than frowning. And it's more powerful. When you smile, it's like pushing a button and activating a response. The person you smile at almost always smiles back.

One of my favorite songs about smiling dates back to a silent movie that came out in 1936. Some of you were born the year Charlie Chaplin appeared in *Modern Times.* Some of you were youngsters and went to see it at the local show palace.

Did you realize that the song *SMILE* was actually written by Charlie Chaplin? Inspired by the music of Puccini, the millionaire tramp wrote the lyric-less tune that was used as part of the film's soundtrack. Two decades later, John Turner and Geoffrey Parsons collaborated on the lyrics.

Smile, though your heart is aching
Smile, even though it's breaking
When there are clouds in the sky
you'll get by

If you smile through your fear and sorrow
Smile and maybe tomorrow
You'll see the sun come shining through
for you

Light up your face with gladness
Hide every trace of sadness
Although a tear may be ever so near

That's the time you must keep on trying
Smile what's the use of crying
You'll find that life is still worthwhile
If you'll just smile.

Jimmy Durante and Nat King Cole made the Charlie Chaplin tune famous. So did the King of Pop, Michael Jackson.

The writer of Proverbs went on record as saying, *A merry heart does good like medicine.* (Proverbs 17:22) It's quite possible he was smiling as he wrote those timeless words. I'm guessing a merry heart also included a smiling face.

It is possible (and healthy) to smile when your heart is aching and breaking because you know you'll eventually get by. Choosing to find joy and hope in the midst of pain and grief is a good thing.

But the bad thing is pretending to be happy when you're not. I hate the line in the song, *Hide every trace of sadness.* Hiding your honest feelings is dishonest. Stuffing grief and ignoring heartache is a recipe for disaster.

Wearing a mask to prevent the spread of COVID is not the same thing as wearing an invisible emotional mask that denies what's going on in your heart. A merry heart and a grieving heart are not mutually exclusive. Laughter and tears are Siamese twins that live in the same chamber of the soul. The key is smiling through the pain while still acknowledging what hurts. It's only when we admit we are having a tough time that others can comfort us. And that includes being open and honest with God.

Do not cast me from your presence or take your Holy Spirit from me. Restore to me the joy of your salvation and grant me a willing spirit, to sustain me. (Psalm 51:11-12)

68

Do you ever get thirsty for an old-fashioned chocolate malt? You know the kind I'm referring to? So rich and thick that it hurts your cheeks to suck that icy-cold chocolatey goodness through the straw. Well, I know exactly where to find one.

The Owl Soda Fountain in my hometown of Wenatchee has been my favorite watering hole since I was twelve years old. The rotating stools with bright red seats, the black and white checkerboard tile floor, the enamel green milkshake mixers, the black hard-rubber knobs the soda jerk pulls to squirt soda water into the brown chocolate syrup ... it's just as you remember from your youth.

Oh, and did I mention they still have a juke box in the corner that plays? Talk about happy days!

Most every summer and fall for the past seven years, I've escorted residents from our campus on a day trip to The Owl Soda Fountain. There's something about The Owl that reminds me of simpler days. It's a counter-culture (literally) that calls to mind a less-stressful, easy-going time when faith, patriotism and community spirit took precedence over political ideologies or concern for political correctness.

Those were the days when Sundays were distinctive from the other six days of the week. And sundaes at the local soda shop were the reward for getting good grades on a report card.

Obviously, there's no way of going back to the way things were in the fifties. The horse is out of the barn and the barn and the farm have been replaced by single-family homes in a suburban subdivision.

But there is a way of recapturing a God-focus where we take time to begin each day and end each day mindful of One who longs to refresh us with a sense of His presence and sweeten our perspective of a world in chaos that often leaves us with a bitter taste in our mouths.

It was the psalmist who wrote: *Taste and see that the LORD is good; blessed is the one who takes refuge in him.* (Psalm 34:8)

While the Owl Soda Fountain may be the perfect place to get a quick fix for a refreshing treat on a hot summer day, refreshment for our souls requires getting back to basics and finding our perspective in God's presence and God's Word instead of *FOX* or *CNN.*

69

My middle daughter got married to her pastor-husband in the summer of 2011. Since that day they exchanged vows, God has blessed them with a home, a church and two precious little girls by the names of Imogen and Ivy.

I'll never forget the day Allison and Tim pledged a lifetime of love to each other on the campus of North Park College and Seminary. It was just shy of 100 degrees, but fortunately Anderson Chapel was air-conditioned. As the father of the bride, I was called on to wear two hats that day. I walked my daughter down the aisle and then turned around to officiate the ceremony.

Since I had proposed to Allison's mom on a Scrabble board (and since playing Scrabble has always been a huge part of our family), I used a Scrabble board to illustrate words that describe a lifelong commitment in my wedding homily. The words on the board spelled out what it takes to make a marriage last.

Think about it. A healthy marriage requires any number of qualities. It takes time, honesty, forgiveness. It takes grit and grace. It takes faith, hope and love. But it also takes humor and patience and trust.

Commitment is the result of more than simply making a vow. Saying "I do" isn't enough. Love does.

We often hear 1 Corinthians 13 (commonly called the love chapter) read at a wedding. In fact, I read it at a wedding I conducted last weekend. But Paul wasn't referring to a couple pledging marital vows when he originally wrote *Love is patient and kind. It always perseveres.*

He was calling Christians to love one another in a context of commitment. He was prescribing a way of life that will keep relationships from dying. He was offering a vaccine that will prevent us losing those we love through unnecessary misunderstandings or regrettable mistakes.

For Saint Paul, the same words apply for you and me as for a starry-eyed couple at the front of a church. Trust. Honesty. Forgiveness. Grit and grace.

That's what makes for meaningful relationships that will carry us through the unpredictable challenges of life.

Love does not delight in evil but rejoices with the truth. It always protects, always trusts, always hopes, always perseveres. (1 Corinthians 13:6-7)

70

How long will this pandemic ultimately last? Who knows? How long, indeed!

How long? is a question that the people of God have asked throughout history. In Psalm 13:1-2, we read:

> *How long, LORD? Will you forget me forever?*
> *How long will you hide your face from me?*
> *How long must I wrestle with my thoughts*
> *and day after day have sorrow in my heart?*
> *How long will my enemy triumph over me?*

In the short space of two verses, the psalmist asks four times, *How long?*

We, like the writer of Psalm 13, are ready to be done. It's been long enough, already! Right? It's time we get back to normal.

It reminds me of vacation road trips with my three girls when they were young. *Are we there yet, Daddy?* Remember those days? No matter how thoroughly you stuffed their backpacks and packed the kids' suitcases, there never was enough patience for them.

We all long to be back to normal. And speaking of normal, several years ago my friend, Ken, and his wife, Carol, were planning a trip to Illinois. After flying from Seattle and spending some time with friends in Chicagoland, they were going to rent a car and drive to Normal, Illinois. Because Ken knew Wendy and I had raised our family near the Windy City, he called me and asked, "How long will it take to get to Normal?"

And speaking of normal, what a great question for these days in which we find ourselves. But the answer is not quite as obvious as the one I gave my friend. If only we could get back to normal quickly, back to those summer road trips.

When I was a kid and my dad was in the driver's seat, I remember countless trips to Idaho, to Oregon and California where there always seemed to be road crews working on the highways. We'd have to stop and wait for what seemed like hours. And then a pilot car would come and lead the procession of cars that went on for what seemed like miles. Not a happy memory of childhood road trips. Why? Because I hated the state of waiting. Idaho? Oregon? California? Washington? All beautiful states. But not the state of waiting.

Realistically, we need to find the beauty in the waiting state. We'd do well to enjoy this unpopular state as a time to reflect. That's what the psalmist did. He concludes his psalm with these words:

But I trust in your unfailing love;
my heart rejoices in your salvation.
I will sing the LORD's praise,
for he has been good to me.

Maybe that's a good suggestion for us. While we wait and wonder how long, let's think back on God's goodness and take grateful stock in what God has already accomplished on our behalf.

71

The year of 2020 found us mourning the deaths of many celebrities. Within a short span of time we lost Congressman John Lewis, actress Olivia de Haviland, and television personality Regis Philbin.

Speaking of Regis, I first saw him in person in Hollywood when I was sixteen years old. It was the summer of 1968 and our family was vacationing in Southern California.

After stopping at the Ambassador Hotel where Robert Kennedy had recently been assassinated, we checked in at a motel in Hollywood.

After dinner my brother and I walked by the ABC studios where *The Joey Bishop Show* was about to be taped. Who should stroll by but Regis and Joey? I've been a fan of Regis ever since.

I loved his show with Kathie Lee Gifford, and then the one with Kelly Rippa. But I think my favorite Regis show was *Who Wants to Be a Millionaire?*

It's with that show in mind (and hoping that Regis was prepared for his "final answer" when he stood before the Judge), that I wrote this poetic tribute.

"Who wants to be a millionaire?"
he asked. And we were game.
Who wouldn't want to win at trivia?

147

But even Regis knew deep down
that riches can't buy life
when comes that day when we must say "See ya!"

No! Phone-a-friend won't do the trick
no matter who we know.
Sweet Kathie Lee or Kelly won't suffice.
When we must stand before the Lord
and brace for what's in store,
our final answer can't be "I was nice!"

For Regis (or for anyone)
the rules are all the same.
The only lifeline we can claim is grace.
The good we've done or our success
won't matter in the end.
It all comes down to Whom we have embraced.

Trivia? Oh, by no means.
This is the Gospel truth.
God's grace through faith is that by which we win.
The "Game of Life" continues on
beyond our final breath.
So use your lifeline now and trust in Him.

For by grace we have been saved through faith; and that not of ourselves.
It is a gift of God lest anyone should boast. (Ephesians 2:8-9)

72

Last week one of our residents shared a photo with me. It's a picture of a black bird's nest with eggs in it. The nest is just outside her apartment on our campus. It's beautiful. But more than simply being beautiful, according to Mary Lu, it pictures hope.

There is just something about new life that speaks of hope, right? In our backyard there have been several baby bunnies hopping around early in the morning and late in the afternoon. They are so cute. But the damage they do to my wife's garden is not all that adorable.

Nonetheless, bird eggs and baby bunnies are signs that life goes on. Who was it who said, *Babies are God's way of saying He hasn't given up on the world?* I love that expression. And with grandbabies invading our previously empty nest on Lansdowne Lane, I can readily identify with the sentiment. God has much more in store. There is reason to hope. We have cause to trust.

In a COVID world that is complicated by violence and riots wreaking havoc on our cities, hope is hard to come by. Some might say the evening news is for the birds. Squawk, squawk, squawk.

Did you know that some say the 81st psalm is for the birds as well? Literally. It's a psalm that recalls the Lord's deliverance of His people from bondage. It celebrates God's provision during "iffy" times. It documents the disobedience of those who should have been gratefully compliant. It underscores the longsuffering lovingkindness of a God who refuses to give up on His people.

Near the end of the passage we read these words:

I am the LORD *your God,*
  who brought you up out of Egypt.
Open wide your mouth and I will fill it.

Did you know those words are a direct reference to nature? It's a picture that we have seen in person or on the Animal Planet channel. When a mama bird flies to the nest with a worm in her mouth, her young open their mouths wide to be fed. It's a beautiful image that pictures God's desire to provide for our needs and nourish us with His love.

Why not personalize that verse from Psalm 81?
I am the LORD *your God,*
  who brought you through COVID.
Open wide your mouth and I will fill it.

Opening our mouths begins with opening our hearts and acknowledging our dependence on a Higher Power.

73

Normally, this is the time of the year when kids begin to think about returning to school. But this year *back to school* does not mean *back to normal*. Will it be in-person classes or virtual or a combination of both? Who knows? It depends who you ask and who you ask seems to change their tune week to week. It also depends on what part of the country you live in.

As a kid, I remember bemoaning the fact that summer vacation was coming to an end and the start of school was looming. It was not a happy thought.

But there was something about the end of summer vacation that actually did spark interest for me. It was back-to-school shopping. Teachers would communicate with parents the list of items needed to be purchased. In elementary school that meant new boxes of crayons, three ring binders, notebook paper, gym shoes. In fifth grade we had to have a ballpoint pen to use for spelling tests. Practice tests on Thursdays were done in pencil. But the final test on Fridays had to be taken with ink. No erasures allowed!

There was something about shopping for brand new school supplies that was exciting. And Mom would always spring for new school clothes. A new pair of Levis and shoes. Were they Keds? Buster Browns? Converse? I frankly can't remember.

Back-to-school shopping trips triggered positive emotions. I guess it was the joy of starting over. A fresh start is definitely a biblical concept.

It was St. Paul who modeled for us the positive practice of forgetting what is behind and straining forward to what is ahead. *The old is gone. The new is here.* (2 Corinthians 5:17)

Every morning is an invitation to start over and begin anew. It's kind of like a blank slate. The following variation of the *Serenity Prayer* celebrates the fresh starts God's grace makes possible:

A blank slate? Yes! Amazing grace
has cleansed my past. It's been erased.
The present is God's gift to me
to learn from my mistakes.

So, help me, God, to make today
a brand new start. And so I pray
that You would guide me as I go
to do the things I should.

Serenity. I ask of You.
Accepting what I can't undo.
And wisdom so to understand
what (bravely) I can change.

74

Most Seattle-ites recall the name Pat O'Day. He was for many years the voice of *KJR Seattle (Channel 95)*. A beloved deejay and a concert promoter, Pat was the man at the mic for SeaFair hydroplane races. He was born Paul Berg to a Tacoma pastor and his wife. His brother, Dave Berg, spent his career teaching at a Christian school in the Seattle area.

Pat O'Day reached the summit of success early in his life, and like many who find that mountaintop less fulfilling than they had hoped, he became addicted to alcohol and drugs. In recent years Pat became a spokesperson promoting the virtues of Schick Shadel Recovery Programs. Having become a patient, he was so impressed with the results that he became an owner of the company.

One of my best friends worked for Pat O'Day back in the day. George called to tell me that Pat was near death. But he also told me that Pat had recently recommitted his life to Christ and was ready to go home. It's with that background that I share with you a tribute to Pat O'Day. It's simply called *Remembering the Voice of Channel 95*.

This summer day began quite gray
while hearing Pat had passed away.
The voice of Channel 95
has signed off one last time.

This rock promoter's unique sound
broke barriers. He broke new ground.

O'Day (like Dick Clark) had a way
of spinning vinyl gold.

A pastor's kid, Pat loved his dad.
He loved God, too, but Pat was rad.
He found success and lost his way
for way too many years.

He came to know the stars by name.
Intoxicated by his fame,
Pat stumbled forward with the hope
he'd gain what mattered most.

The drugs and booze would take their toll,
but in the end Pat knew his soul
belonged to One who gave His life
to set the captive free.

Pat left this world while pointing to
the Savior who had made him new.
The one-time king of KJR
has claimed a lasting crown.

75

I don't know about you, but I'm generally always thirsty for a fresh cup of hot coffee. That's my drink of choice. I'm a coffee connoisseur. I have my first cup about 6:30 in the morning and keep sipping the nectar of the gods throughout the day. It doesn't matter how hot it is outside. I love hot coffee. It should be noted, I hate lukewarm coffee.

Recently I discovered that the decanter in the staff lounge wasn't keeping the coffee hot. I wasted no time in requesting we get a new container. There's nothing worse than tepid coffee. Tepid coffee is terrible coffee (even if it costs $2 a cup at the local St. Arbucks).

I'm guessing after today's devotion I'll have a new nickname. Instead of Chappy G, you just might start calling me Mr. Coffee or Chaplain Folgers.

Speaking of names, our names are very significant. Our names signify our reputation. I love that line from Shakespeare's play, *Othello*, where Iago says, *Who steals my purse steals trash. But he who robs me of my good name takes that which profits him nothing, but without which I am poor indeed.*

The story is told of Alexander the Great. One day he sat upon his throne, pronouncing sentences for the crimes charged to his soldiers. The sergeant-at-arms brought in one soldier after another and read their crimes. No one could escape from Alexander's severe judgments.

Finally, the sergeant-at-arms brought in a young Macedonian soldier and read aloud his crime: "Fleeing in the face of the enemy."

Alexander the Great was known as one who could not tolerate cowardice. But as he looked on this young soldier, the monarch's countenance changed from stern to soft.

Smiling, he said to the lad, "Son, what is your name?" The boy said softly, "Alexander."

The smile left the king's face. "What did you say?" he demanded.

The young man snapped to attention. "Alexander, sir!"

The king turned crimson and shouted, "WHAT IS YOUR NAME?"

The boy began to stammer and said, "Al-Alex-Alexander, sir!"

The king burst out of his chair, grabbed the young man by the tunic, stared him in the face, then threw him on the ground and said, "Soldier, change your conduct or change your name!"

Those of us who acknowledge Christ as our Lord and Savior have a lineage to live up to. We've been given a royal name.

What is your name? Christian? Really? Then we'd best live our lives in a manner worthy of that name.

76

In the summer of 2005 our family arrived on Mercer Island, an island connected to downtown Seattle by a floating bridge. We had moved from Naperville, Illinois.

To paraphrase astronaut Neil Armstrong, *Moving to this foot-shaped island …*

By the way, did you know that Mercer Island is shaped like a foot? Now you do. Anyway …

Moving to this foot-shaped island was at once one small step and a giant leap for me.

It was a small step because I knew the island. My grandfather had built a home on the island in the fifties. My uncle and aunt had lived here since the seventies. Bud Palmberg, the former pastor for the church I had been called to serve, had been my Monday golfing buddy when I first entered the ministry forty years ago.

Moving back to the area was also a giant leap. It was a return to fulltime pastoral ministry after working as a fulltime freelance writer. It was a return to the Pacific Northwest after having lived in other parts of the country for a quarter century (and Seattle had definitely changed from my years as a bachelor-pastor).

It was a return to where my life had begun with the full knowledge that my dad was terminally ill with metastatic prostate cancer and I wasn't sure how much time I'd have with him.

Small steps. Giant leaps. Our lives are defined by small steps and giant leaps. Each day we have routine activities that we tackle without thinking. We call those kinds of activities no-brainers.

But then there are the bigger challenges that this season in our lives thrusts our way. Challenges of health, finances, separation from family and memory loss. Without doubt we'd have to acknowledge that the coronavirus (and all the ways it additionally complicates our lives) is a giant king of challenge.

Like Armstrong's tentative steps on the surface of the moon, we aren't quite sure how steady our footing will be or what to expect when we step out of bed each morning. We think we have an idea of what the day will hold, but we can't be entirely sure.

I take comfort (and courage) from what the Bible says: *We can make our plans, but the LORD determines our steps.* (Proverbs 16:9)

The key, it seems to me, is asking the Lord to give us the ability to trust His sovereign will a day at a time. Both our small steps and giant leaps are in God's hands.

77

It was on August 10, 1897 that a German chemist by the name of Felix Hoffman first synthesized acetylsalicylic acid. Never heard of it? Of course you have. The Bayer company for which Felix Hoffman worked would later patent acetylsalicylic acid under its household name "aspirin."

What kind of a world would it be if doctors were never heard to say, *Take a couple aspirin and call me in the morning?* How often have we benefited from those two little white pills?

I have a good friend who is alive today because he chewed an aspirin some twelve years ago when he was in the process of having a stroke. It was like a miracle. What my friend had once been told actually worked.

Do you remember the tag line for Bayer aspirin? *Bayer works wonders!* For years it was known as the wonder drug.

But lest we give Felix Hoffman's employer too much credit, that sentiment was not original with the Bayer company. Long before aspirin, God owned that tagline. The One we worship is the One who works wonders. The Lord of life is the Lord of all. He does wonderful things. His name is wonderful. He is a wonderful counselor, everlasting Father and the prince of peace.

And this wonderful God is the Great Physician. When we are sick, we head for an urgent-care facility or perhaps contact our physician with a video call. In an emergency, we call 911. But we should always call out to our Sovereign Lord. In Him we live and move and have our very being. Ours is a God who welcomes our calls for help.

Come unto me all you who are burdened and I will give you rest. (Matthew 11:28)

You know that passage from the Bible? Of course, you do. It's our invitation to call out to a God who knows our need and has our very best interest at heart.

Even when we're not physically sick, but just emotionally stressed, we should "take 2." Pause and pray. Take a deep breath and from the depths of your heart admit your need to the All-Seeing God who monitors your every move. Take 2 and call on God in the morning and at night. In fact, why not call on Him right now?

78

Have you ever wondered where the name August comes from? Would you believe the eighth month of the year is in honor of Caesar Augustus? According to St. Luke's Gospel, Augustus was emperor of the Roman Empire when Jesus was born. (And just for the record, July is named for Julius Caesar, the general and Roman statesman who lived just prior to Augustus.)

I like the name Augustus. It has a regal sound to it. It means majestic or venerable. Curiously it's a family name. My paternal grandmother's older brother was Thomas Augustus Turley.

I met my Uncle Tom when I was twelve years old. This grocer-turned-farmer and his wife (Miss Mae) traveled from their home in Wytheville, Virginia to Spaulding, Idaho for a visit with my grandmother.

I was impressed with my great-uncle. He was kind. He was debonair. And he wasn't very tall. We were about the same height. Also, I loved his southern drawl.

Even though he was a rather short man, there was much about him to love. Like his middle name implied, Uncle Tom was a noble respectable southern gentleman.

That summer of 1963 was the only time I got to spend with my Great-Uncle Tom. He died some thirty years ago. But I did have the good fortune of getting to know his son, Thomas Augustus, Jr. We called him "T.A." And in recent months I've begun connecting via email with T.A.'s son, Thomas Augustus III. Although he goes by Tom, when he was a kid he was known as "Auggie."

Your name might not be as august a name as that of my great-uncle, but it's important. It's the name your parents gave you. The mention of your name to those who know you calls to mind more than your face. Your name is a representation of who you are and what you stand for. Your name equals your reputation.

In Proverbs 22:1 we read, *A good name is more desirable than great riches*. In other words, our name is more valuable than our savings account, our cash on hand or a debit card. Our name is the best credit rating we could hope for.

That is, of course, if it's a good name. Every day of our lives we have the opportunity to improve our credit score. From sun up to sun down we have a chance to align our behavior with our core values. Each day is a chance to revise our reputation.

79

I love to walk, don't you? And if you are currently unable to walk like you used to, I'm guessing you can't really stand your immobility.

For the past two years, Wendy and I have made it a priority to walk three miles four days a week. We love to walk at the start of the day through a forest near our home on Mercer Island. Walking clears our heads and lubricates our joints. It's a good way to rehearse our personal agendas. It's a meaningful way to begin the day.

My friend, Diane Medved, is a regular columnist in a monthly periodical called *Mercer Island Living*. A recent column by Diane is called *The Joy of Walking*.

In her article, Diane celebrates the benefits associated with walking. Walking can help control your weight. It can prevent heart disease and certain cancers. It can improve your mental attitude. In addition, if socially distanced, walking with a friend allows you to maintain relationships while staying fit.

Diane concludes her column with a quote by Charles Dickens:

Walk and be happy. Walk and be healthy. The best way to lengthen out our days is to walk — steadily and with a purpose.

Diane's husband, Michael, is often seen walking with a purpose in my neighborhood. He carries a grabber and a large garbage bag. He has a penchant for picking up litter in a focused attempt to keep this corner of God's green earth beautiful.

Knowing the Medveds as I do, I know that they would also attest to the fact that walking has a spiritual component. As observant Jews, the Medveds walk three miles to the local synagogue and three back home each Sabbath. In the process, they experience the presence of the Creator while honoring the Fourth Commandment.

We are blest to have a walking path along the lake where I work. Our staff and residents alike can experience the presence of the Creator with magnificent vistas. Even during COVID I watched as housebound survivors took advantage of our scenic path. Our lakeside loop provides a perfect opportunity to talk the Lord while taking a walk.

As you exercise your body, you can exercise your faith. What we often refer to as our walk with God can actually be enriched by stepping out and taking a walk.

Did you notice I said, "Taking a walk" instead of "Going for a walk"? That was purposeful. You see, a walk in the great outdoors is yours for the taking. It's a gift ready to be opened and enjoyed. Go ahead and claim it today.

80

As a seventeen-year-old I faced a judge in court, nervously anticipating the verdict. I hadn't broken any law and I wasn't accused of any crime. So what was I doing in the courtroom? No, I wasn't on a jury. I was too young for that. And I should add that I wasn't standing before the judge all alone. My mom and dad and brother were standing with me.

The reason we were there was to petition the courts to have our name legally changed from *Smith* to *Asimakoupoulos*. Seven decades earlier my paternal grandfather had emigrated from Greece. He was so proud of his new adopted country he wanted to change his name. He wanted an American name. So Haralambos Athanasius Asimakoupoulos became Harry Kenneth Smith.

Harry married Margaret Turley from Wytheville, VA and together they raised six kids in the panhandle of Idaho. There was Irene, Elaine, Billy, Edwin and the twins Louise and Lois. The Smith kids grew up and married. Edwin Smith married Star Birkeland and they had two sons: Greg and Marc.

But as Edwin had the opportunity to meet and spend time with relatives in Greece, he grew to regret the fact that his father had surrendered his European name. In spite of the paperwork and expense of the process, Edwin decided to undo what his dad had done. And so on August 13, 1969, my father legally changed our last name to what it was at first.

I was just going into my senior year of high school. It's a day I will never forget and it's a decision for which I will always be grateful.

I'm guessing you might relate. You see, we all share a grandfather by the name of Adam. He was a professional gardener. A long time ago in a place far away, he changed his name from *sinless son of God* to *father of flawed humanity*.

Ever since being expelled from Eden, we and our relatives have been tempted to retain our alias rather than claim our original identity and change our name back.

St. Paul said it succinctly: *If anyone is in Christ, they are a new creation. The old is past the new has come.* (2 Corinthians 5:17)

81

Remember Joe Friday? That was Jack Webb's character on the old TV series *Dragnet*. Wendy and I recently got hooked binge watching a Masterpiece Mystery series on PBS called *Endeavor*. One of the main characters is a detective by the name of Fred Thursday.

Speaking of Thursday, yesterday we talked about names. Today I want to talk about nicknames. Nicknames are huge even though we may not like the nicknames we were given as kids.

Because my mom was the baby of the family, she became known as Babe. Because my dad was quite outspoken about his faith in high school, his classmates called him Preacher. Meanwhile, my dad's father (the Greek immigrant) rarely called him Edwin (his given name). My grandfather called my dad Nick. Why Nick? Well, if you've ever seen *My Big Fat Greek Wedding*, you'd realize how many Greek men are referred to as Nick.

When I was a kid, my last name was Smith. As a result, I was called Smitty. After we changed our name, I became Ozzie. Today at my place of employment, I am known as Chappy G.

I have a nickname for each of our kids. Kristin is Krissy Nick. Allison is Ally Bug. And Lauren is Lor Lor.

What were you called as a kid? Kate? Sugar? Sweet Pea? Peg? Bunny? Slim? Honey? Jackson? Tex?

Did you know that being given a nickname is an indication that you are loved? Nicknames convey an emotional connection and recognized accessibility. A short name or nickname is a sign of intimacy, trust, and friendship.

Jesus gave nicknames to some of the disciples: Simon was known as Peter (or a better translation would be Rocky). James and John, the hot-tempered brothers were called "Sons of Thunder." Another of the disciples was referred to as "the Zealot."

What do you think Jesus would have called you? I think I have an idea.

Back when I was in college, a devotional came out written by Frances Roberts. It was titled *Come Away My Beloved*. Much like the popular current book *Jesus Calling*, *Come Away My Beloved* was written as though it is the Lord speaking directly to you.

And believe me, you are the Lord's beloved. You are loved. You are forgiven. You are special.

Remember that unforgettable promise found in the Old Testament? *"I know the plans I have for you," declares the Lord. "Plans for good and not for evil, to give you a future and a hope."* (Jeremiah 29:11).

82

Speaking of real, I had a hard time getting into the reduced 60-game major league baseball schedule. Any hopes for a normal season was thrown out at home. And thanks to COVID, home was the only way to catch a game. Somehow watching games from empty stadiums didn't cut it. Cardboard cutout fans in the stands and artificial piped-in crowd noise left me less than satisfied. True, the players are really on the field. But it just didn't seem real. There was just too much pretend in this version of the game to capture my passion for the game.

So what is real? That's a great question. I love that section from Marjorie Williams' classic children's book, *The Velveteen Rabbit*, where that very question is asked. Maybe you remember this scene:

"What is REAL?" asked the Rabbit one day, when they were lying side by side near the nursery fender, before Nana came to tidy the room. "Does it mean having things that buzz inside you and a stick-out handle?"

"Real isn't how you are made," said the Skin Horse. "It's a thing that happens to you. When a child loves you for a long, long time, not just to play with, but REALLY loves you, then you become Real."

"Does it hurt?" asked the Rabbit.

"Sometimes," said the Skin Horse, for he was always truthful. "When you are Real you don't mind being hurt."

"Does it happen all at once, like being wound up," he asked, "or bit by bit?"

"It doesn't happen all at once," said the Skin Horse. "You become. It takes a long time. That's why it doesn't happen often to people who break easily, or have sharp edges, or who have to be carefully kept. Generally, by the time you are Real, most of your hair has been loved off, and your eyes drop out and you get loose in the joints and very shabby. But these things don't matter at all, because once you are Real you can't be ugly, except to people who don't understand."

"I suppose you are real?" said the Rabbit. And then he wished he had not said it, for he thought the Skin Horse might be sensitive. But the Skin Horse only smiled.

Real is all about being genuine and loving without concern for what other people think. It's exactly what the Pharisees were not. That's why Jesus was so hard on them. They were professional pretenders. Doing religious things and saying religious-sounding things and praying pious prayers for the benefit of others.

Christianity is a religion that encourages being real. Admitting our need. Admitting our faults. Admitting our fears.

It's a religion that embraces what is real and looks to a God who really responds.

Cast all your anxiety on Him (God) for He cares for you. (1 Peter 5:7)

83

So, who is Cal Ripken, you ask? Well, for those of you who don't know, he was an all-star major league baseball player for the Baltimore Orioles.

What is most notable about Cal Ripken is that he broke a record long held by Lou Gehrig of playing in the most number of baseball games without a break. On September 6, 1995, Cal Ripken suited up and played in his 2,131st straight game. Can you imagine? When you consider that the typical number of games in a regular season is 162, that's a lot of years without missing a game.

In a COVID season like this, major league baseball teams are playing only sixty games. But 162 games year after year, that's a lot of suiting up to play without sitting out.

There is something to be said for dependability. Dependability is a virtue that employers value. It's a virtue that represents a sense of responsibility and obligation.

Sadly, in our day dependability is not a virtue that is demonstrated among the younger generation as it was when we were growing up. We were taught that others are depending on us. That we have a role to play that no one else can fill.

While doing what needs to be done can leave us feeling tired or unappreciated, that is no reason to refuse to take the field. The payoff for staying at the plate and facing the curve balls life throws at us is at the end of the game. Too often we wonder whether what we are doing really matters or if it's really making a difference. Such ponderings are premature. We just need to keep doing good until the third out in the bottom of the ninth.

Let us not become weary in doing good, for at the proper time we will reap a harvest if we do not give up. (Galatians 6:9)

84

Did you know that the shortest war in history took place on August 27 1896? It took only thirty-eight minutes for Great Britain to defeat the Zanzibar Sultanate. Wow! Only thirty-eight minutes.

Speaking of short. Did you ever hear of the *One-Day Governor*? His name was Samuel Cosgrove. Governor Cosgrove was the sixth chief executive of the State of Washington. He suffered a heart attack while giving his inaugural address on January 27, 1909.

Before being elected, Cosgrove practiced law in the eastern Washington community of Pomeroy, as well as managing 1400 acres of farm land in Washington and Idaho. He was president of the Pomeroy School Board for eight years and served as Pomeroy's mayor for five terms.

I was delighted to discover that Samuel Cosgrove had a connection to the campus where I work. Governor Cosgrove's granddaughter was a resident here when I was called to be chaplain of Covenant Living at the Shores. Myrne Philbrick was an elegant woman who allowed me the privilege of helping her pack her bags for Heaven.

As I spent time with Myrne, I learned that her other grandfather was a rather well-known Washington pioneer as well. Captain George Kinnear earned an enviable reputation as a land developer in the burgeoning city of Seattle in the late 1880s.

Against the backdrop of the shortest war in history and the shortest term a governor ever served, I'd like to suggest one more. How about short-lived resentment? How well do you do in that department? It is said of one of the candidates running for president in the most recent election, "He doesn't hold grudges."

Wouldn't it be great if that could be said of all of us? Do you think that is what our Heavenly Father expects?

In Ephesians 4:26 we read: *Be angry and don't sin. Don't let the sun go down on your wrath.*

In other words, keep short accounts. Forgive and move on. Holding on to resentment has been compared to drinking poison and hoping the other person dies.

Let's hear it for short-lived resentments!

85

While visiting a cemetery in Southern California recently, I was contemplating the brevity of life and the certainty of death. I was also reminded of the price tag associated with the freedoms I enjoy as an American. But in the midst of a global pandemic, I found myself praying that peace might become a reality in our war-ravaged world.

As I walked among the grave markers, I found one belonging to Corrie ten Boom. I paused and thanked the Lord for this precious one whose remains lay beneath a simple granite tombstone. Corrie's autobiography is called *The Hiding Place*. Perhaps you read this remarkable book. I hope so.

Three quarters of a century ago the Nazis occupied the Netherlands. A Dutch watchmaker with his young family practiced his own version of sheltering in place. Papa ten Boom hid his Jewish neighbors in a secret compartment in his multistoried home. It was more than social distancing. It was lifesaving. It was Christ-honoring. It was putting his faith into practice.

If you know Corrie ten Boom's story, you know that the Gestapo eventually discovered the hiding place and carted off the Christian family and their Jewish friends to concentration camps. When the allied forces freed the camps in 1945, Corrie was the only survivor of her group.

Half a century ago, I had the privilege of introducing Corrie ten Boom as the guest speaker at Seattle Pacific University. I was moved by her faith journey then and I continue to be today. Her courageous God-focused desire to stand up against injustice while risking one's own freedom and safety is an example to us all.

It was Jesus who said, *Greater love has no one than this that they lay down their life for their friends.* (John 15:13)

86

Do you know the name Gale Sayers? He was a former NFL player known for his designation as the youngest person to ever be inducted into the Pro Football Hall of Fame. Gale played college football at the University of Kansas before being drafted by the Chicago Bears in 1965 and later named Rookie of the Year. Gale Sayers passed away this year.

In his 1970 autobiography, he chronicled how he catapulted himself out of an Omaha ghetto to become one of the greatest running backs in National Football League history. The book also describes his endearing friendship with Chicago Bears teammate Brian Piccolo, who died of cancer.

Gale, an African American, and Brian, his white teammate, were bosom buddies. They encouraged each other when both were having physical issues.

In the story of his life, Sayers described his *I Am Third* philosophy of life. God is first, others are second, and I am third.

When John the Baptist was confronted with how the crowds were following his cousin Jesus, he didn't have a pity party or have an envy fueled anxiety attack. Rather, he said, *He must increase and I must decrease.* (John 3:30)

How could he say that? Obviously, his vision for life was based on a Godward focus that enabled him to see clearly. He understood that the most fulfilling life possible is rooted in putting others ahead of oneself.

When I attended Sunday school in my pastor-father's church sixty years ago, the teacher led us in a little song that illustrated the truth both Gale Sayers and John the Baptist bought into.

It went like this:
Jesus and others and you.
What a wonderful way to spell joy.
Jesus and others and you
in the life of each girl and each boy.
J is for Jesus for he has first place.
O is for others you meet face to face.
Y is for you in whatever you do.
Put yourself third and spell joy.

Humble yourselves before the Lord, and He will lift you up. (James 4:10)

87

Hello Americans. Stand by for news!

That's how the late and much-loved radio commentator Paul Harvey began each newscast each day for fifty-six years.

A highlight in my adult life was sitting in on one of Paul Harvey's newscasts from his studio in downtown Chicago. Several years later I randomly met Mr. Harvey while vacationing in Phoenix. The place where we stayed was located in the same subdivision of the celebrated newscaster.

I recognized Mr. Harvey out for a stroll on the sidewalk and took the initiative to introduce myself to him. I asked if I could join him. We walked and talked for about twenty minutes. I had the opportunity to thank him for his contribution to our nation through his thoughtful commentaries. Recognizing he was in frail health, I asked if I could pray over him. I will forever be grateful I was assertive.

One of the things that distinguished Paul Harvey from other newscasters was his penchant to share good news stories. He didn't just share headlines. He gave us the rest of the story.

You and I may not be currently licensed to work for a radio station, but we have the opportunity to share good news. In spite of the negativity that is headlining our current culture, we can look for the good around us and talk about it.

While our neighbors are standing by for the nightly news, we can make reference to how the good Lord has answered prayer in our lives. We can share with others what gives us optimism in a season of pessimism. We can offer hopeful insights in these uncertain times.

It was the prophet Isaiah who broadcast this message long ago: *How beautiful on the mountains are the feet of those who bring good news, who proclaim peace, who bring good tidings, who proclaim salvation, who say to Zion, "Your God reigns!"* (Isaiah 52:7)

It's a timeless message this is as current now as then.

88

Back when you were employed fulltime, Labor Day was a day off to contemplate with thanksgiving the privilege of having a job and be grateful you were gainfully employed. It was a day of rest that enabled you to reflect on the good things you've accomplished in your work place.

In the opening pages of our Bible we find God the Creator resting after six days of creation. Everything the Lord spoke into existence was declared to be good. When the Lord created men and women in God's own image, they earned the Lord's valedictory stamp of approval. They were declared to be VERY GOOD.

And then the Scriptures indicate that on the seventh day the Lord rested. That was the original Labor Day. A day off to enjoy the fruit of His labor.

Rest is a good thing. Reflection is a good thing. And even though we sometimes say that a job is not supposed to be enjoyable (and thus we call it work), work is a gift as well. It's a good gift.

On this Labor Day I'm reflecting on a great quote from the late Zenos Hawkinson (a much loved professor at North Park University):

God satisfies our physical hunger with bread,
our thirst with water,
our intellectual curiosity with knowledge,
our loneliness with friends,

our sickness with medicine,
our weariness with sleep
and our strength with labor.

In the only Psalm Moses ever wrote, he included these words: *May the favor of the Lord our God rest on us; establish the work of our hands for us — yes, establish the work of our hands.* (Psalm 90:17)

In other words, the work we have done prior to retirement continues to have a lasting impact and influence. Our labor in many cases has resulted in a legacy that continues to impact people and culture. As we go to prayer today, let's ask the Lord to leverage the work we've done to His glory and the good of others.

89

No matter what day of the week the calendar says today is, it's actually Chooseday. You can choose to call it the best day of the week (so far) or the worst day you've ever lived. The choice is up to you.

Speaking of choices, St. Paul clearly suggests that we have a choice as to how we respond to the cards that life deals us. These words from Philippians 4 are my go-to verses when I feel stressed and overwhelmed by the circumstances of life.

Do not be anxious about anything, but in every situation, by prayer and petition, with thanksgiving, present your requests to God. And the peace of God, which transcends all understanding, will guard your hearts and your minds in Christ Jesus. (Philippians 4:6-7)

Choosing not to be anxious and choosing to off-load our cares to God and choosing to be grateful (which means being a bounty hunter … looking for the sources of bounty in our lives no matter how difficult our present circumstances might be), those are the daily choices that break up the log jam that keeps the peace of God from flowing in our direction.

And notice what the peace of God (which transcends all understanding) accomplishes. It guards our hearts and minds. The Greek word translated *guard* is an athletic term. It means to referee or umpire. God's peace blows the whistle on thoughts we have that aren't in bounds. God's peace tells us to take our base when we feel like we have struck out. God's peace is a reality check on

183

inappropriate thoughts and feelings.

Like a bumper sticker I once saw said, *Don't believe everything you think.*

And speaking of our thought life. Paul goes on to say that we should choose carefully what we fixate on. Why? Because our actions generally are motivated by what they spend our time focused on.

Here's what the apostle says:

Finally, brothers and sisters, whatever is true, whatever is noble, whatever is right, whatever is pure, whatever is lovely, whatever is admirable — if anything is excellent or praiseworthy — think about such things. Whatever you have learned or received or heard from me, or seen in me — put it into practice. And the God of peace will be with you. (Philippians 4:8-9)

90

Were you a middle child? Apparently, there is such a thing as National Middle Child Day. Wendy and I have three daughters. Our middle daughter poked fun at my wife and me on Facebook recently. She pointed out publicly (and assuredly tongue-in-cheek) that we had failed to wish her a Happy Middle Child Day.

Her rebuke was the first I'd ever heard of it. I had no clue such a day even existed. So I felt I needed to respond and defend myself. I wrote a comment underneath her post.

I said, *As a first born I'm oblivious to such things as National Middle Child Day. In fact, when I was a kid I had trouble finding middle C on the piano.*

Did you know that there really is such a thing as middle child syndrome?

Stacy DeBroff, founder of momscentral.com, observed: *Middle kids bemoan their fate as being ignored and often grow resentful of all the parental attention given to the oldest and the baby of the family, and feel short-shifted. The middle child usually has to fight harder for the attention of their parents and therefore crave the family spotlight.*

Oh, my! Guilty as charged. But how were we supposed to have known?

Did you know that middle children typically are the peacemakers among siblings? It most likely is just the functional placement in a family setting where the middle child negotiates and brokers whatever is necessary to bring about calm.

In his famous sermon, Jesus declared, *Blessed are the peacemakers, for they will be called children of God.* (Matthew 5:9)

Indeed. Blessed are the peacemakers. I'm not sure he had middle children in mind or not. My best guess is that he had all of us in mind because that's what it means to be children of God.

We are called to be seekers of peace. In fact the Apostle Paul says we are to "run after peace." Now THAT'S a good daily workout. Running after peace is good for us as well as those who might otherwise be estranged from family and friends. Why don't we lace up our running shoes and seek peace today?

91

This week started out for me with a day off at our family cabin at Lake Chelan. I was sipping my cup of coffee on the deck watching the sun creep over the horizon. It was a beautiful morning. The lake was calm. The sky was blue. A flock of Canada geese flew overhead in V-formation. But before long, the wind began to blow. Steady and strong it blew. I mentioned to Wendy, this kind of wind on a hot summer day is what can result in wildfires. And less than an hour later, I saw black clouds of smoke on the horizon to the east.

Sirens could be heard in the distance. Fire trucks could be seen on the highway. By late afternoon the sky was filled with smoke and ash was landing on the deck. By evening it was difficult to see across the lake.

That unexpected wildfire was a picture to me of how quickly life can change. Circumstances that alter our future develop with little or no warning. The day begins one way and ends quite differently. News of a loved one's diagnosis robs us of our peace. An email out of the blue takes our breath away. A phone call finds us packing a suitcase and heading for the airport.

That's the nature of living on a globe that is punctuated by the unpredictable. That's what Moses had in mind when he wrote these lyrics that characterize our lives. From his pen flowed these words:

They are like the new grass of the morning:

187

In the morning it springs up new,
but by evening it is dry and withered. (Psalm 90:5-6)

What is true of a resort town in Central Washington is true of any old day wherever we are. It starts out one way and ends quite another.

I think it helps when our worldview and our view of Scripture invite us to expect the unexpected. We shouldn't be surprised when the winds of change spread the flames of suffering. That doesn't make God untrustworthy. It just validates the fact that we live in a broken, flawed and tragic-prone world.

The way Moses begins Psalm 90 is what we have to keep in focus. He begins by affirming the fact that the Lord has been our dwelling place from day one until now. It's a call to remember to rely on God as our atmosphere and breathe in deeply, recognizing His presence and available grace. Grace that will enable us to face whatever blows our way.

92

Some of you have read the book by Lisa Beamer, the wife of one of those passengers who perished on Flight 93. The title of her book is *Let's Roll!* It relates the story of her husband Todd, a Wheaton College graduate, who led an assault on the terrorist high jackers in the cockpit. He rallied the other passengers with his two-word expression: *Let's Roll!*

It hardly seems possible that two decades have passed since that tragic Tuesday that caught our nation by surprise.

Nineteen years since 9/11
tore a hole within our soul.
Stole our sense of safety from us
left us reeling. Took a toll.

Changed the way we fly at airports.
Altered how we're screened at games.
Made "Let's roll!" a phrase we ponder
when they read a list of names.

Nineteen years since terror found us
on our knees and unified
as we prayed for God's protection
and in grief for those who died.

As we prayed for those still missing
in the rubble on the ground.
As we grieved with grieving loved ones

when remains were finally found.

Nineteen years since blatant vengeance
joined us at the hip as one.
Blurred the lines that once divided.
Now united fearing none.

One in cause and one in spirit.
Fueled by love of liberty.
Motivated by the lives of
those who died to make us free.

Nineteen years since 9/11
showed us how to be our best.
Showed us how we need each other
when we face a grueling test.

Showed us what our nation can be
if we fight a common foe
and how much we need to trust in
One from whom all blessings flow.

September 11, 2001 found us united as a nation facing a common enemy that caught us by surprise. As we face this current crisis, may God be merciful and find us holding hands (virtually) as we unite in a common cause seeking a virus-free country.

93

The writer of the epistle to the Hebrews pictures an athletic stadium as his words flow without interruption from chapter 11 into chapter 12. It's an overflowing stadium of faith heroes who are watching from the grandstands of heaven even as we run our race of faith.

And I don't think any of us needs to be reminded the race of faith is not a 100-yard dash or a 440 run. It's a life-long marathon. Appropriately, the stadium in Greece that the writer of Hebrews had in mind was the site of the ancient marathon.

A quarter of a century ago I wrote the following tribute to celebrate my in-laws' retirement from Wycliffe Bible Translators. What applies to Hugh and Norma Steven applies to us as well.

When God calls, a gun sounds
and a marathon begins.
A life of service.
A lifetime of measured steps which
(because of the distance to be covered)
takes in stride the potholes along the way.
Disappointment. Tears. Rejection.
Exhaustion. Failure. Loss.

A cross I think He called it.
The One who finished first,
who near the end of His own long-distance race
(though winded) sighed, "I thirst!"

It was what He saw beyond the finish line
that bade Him stay His course.
A faithful finish.
And His Father's proud "well done!"
It's true ... Persistence has its price tags.
But also, its rewards!
Like the rush that comes
when you run through the pain
and find a 'second wind'

But don't forget the hush.
That's another joy in the marathon quest.
That quiet contentment that steadies your steps
on 'a long obedience in the same direction.'
The knowledge that you've been true
to what God called you to do
and to that which you promised you would.

Along the way, you learned endurance,
and in the process, made a difference
for Christ and His Kingdom.
Because of your determination to not give up or in,
there are those throughout this nation (and beyond)
who have heard the call of God and joined the race.

You paced yourself well as you've reached your goal.
And the goal you've attained
is the goal we all seek.
Strong, not weak.
Strong, not wilting.
Not bailing out,
but holding out to the end.
Perseverance.
Persistence.
Going the distance.
Finishing well.

94

Ed Pepple was the winningest high school basketball coach in the state of Washington. He accumulated 953 wins over a 49-year career. For the last fifteen years, I've had the privilege of spending time with him. I discovered there is an item on the menu at a local breakfast spot named for Ed. It's called Coach's Pick. Ed loved eating at the Pancake Corral. I loved eating there with him.

The year Coach Pepple retired, he spoke at the Mercer Island High School Baccalaureate Service. I made note of the advice he offered the graduating seniors. This amazing man, who had tasted his share of success, shared with the graduating seniors (that included my daughter, Lauren) the following life lessons:

Smart people learn from their mistakes.
Smarter people learn from the mistakes of others.

Love your enemies. It will drive them crazy.

If you love your job, it's not work.

There are two ways to be rich. Earn more or desire less.

The best things in life are NOT THINGS.

If Jesus had been asked to speak at a high school baccalaureate service, what do you think he might have shared? I think I know. It's tucked in his most famous sermon found in Matthew 6:19-21:

Do not store up for yourselves treasures on earth, where moths and vermin destroy, and where thieves break in and steal. But store up for yourselves treasures in heaven, where moths and vermin do not destroy, and where thieves do not break in and steal. For where your treasure is, there your heart will be also.

95

Does silence make you feel uncomfortable? Maybe if the silence is unplanned or uninvited it seems awkward. Maybe when someone else calls for silence it's different than when you choose to be quiet.

It's funny, or maybe not so funny, but during these months of sheltering in place we've had a lot of silence compared to what we normally do.

A little peace and quiet can be a welcomed relief under normal circumstances. But in the midst of a pandemic, a piece of quiet can seem to be more like a whole than a piece. Quiet that goes on far too long can be a curse more than a blessing.

The key, it occurs to me, is making productive use of our times of silence. Finding meaning in the stillness. Using the quiet as a purposeful pause in which we marinate on mindfulness. Not wasting time but basting time.

In Psalm 46:10 we hear the voice of our Creator:
Be still and know that I am God.

Isaiah the prophet speaks on behalf of the LORD these words:
In quietness and trust is your strength.

In Ecclesiastes we hear wise King Solomon say:
There is a time to speak and a time to be silent.

In the stillness, in the quiet, in the silence we are more apt to acknowledge what's clambering for our attention. And it's where we are more apt to hear God address our concerns.

Some time back I scrawled these thoughts in my journal:

I poured myself some silence …
an afternoon repast …
a needed brew of emptiness
to pace my race with rats.
Just a simple cup of quiet
to still the noise of grown-up toys
some call technology.

Silence …
Simon says (and Garfunkel too)
That silence has its sounds.
I think I would agree.
It's the whisper of a moment
that's tastier than tea.
It's when I hear
God's still small voice of peace.

96

Eighty-seven-year-old Supreme Court Justice Ruth Bader Ginsberg passed away in the midst of the overcast of COVID. It left our nation feeling quite somber. Regardless of our political affiliations, we found ourselves in the mist of mourning.

This remarkable woman was a pioneer for women's rights. And as the father of three daughters (and grandfather of two granddaughters), I'm grateful for what the "notorious RBG" helped to accomplish. Her efforts have made it possible for my girls to have a level playing field in the market place.

Regardless of whether or not you shared her progressive convictions, you have to agree this woman of Jewish faith was a force with which to be reckoned. Justice Ginsberg was a referee who blew the whistle on longstanding laws in our country that were out of bounds or out of step with the intent of the Constitution.

There was another person of Jewish ancestry who was quite vocal about gender and racial equality. It was a first-century rabbi by the name of Paul of Tarsus who insisted that *In Christ there is neither male nor female.* (Galatians 3:28)

He went on to say that in the Kingdom of God there is no cause to discriminate between Jews or Gentiles. And to think that this rabbi-turned-Christian evangelist claimed to speak on behalf of the Creator.

That said, the Supreme Court of the Cosmos has spoken. God's intention is for the human family to stand on level ground. Different gifts. Different opportunities. Unique responsibilities. Assigned roles. But all equal in God's sight.

"Justice served." Thanks, Justice Ginsberg, for helping to open our culturally blinded eyes corrupted by the cataracts of sin. May we (in our own spheres of influence) seek a more just world by the choices we make, the relationships in which we invest and the words we speak (or refrain from speaking) today.

97

Today I'd like to consider one of the most well-known prayers of all time. No, I'm not referring to the Lord's Prayer. I'm talking about the *Serenity Prayer*. Even if you have heard it and even prayed it many times, consider these familiar words as if for the very first time:

God, grant me the serenity to accept the things I cannot change, courage to change the things I can and wisdom to know the difference.

For the past sixty-five years, that simple prayer of submission has been voiced by countless individuals in twelve-step programs around the world. It was written by a respected theologian during the Great Depression. Reinhold Niebuhr taught at Union Seminary in New York City. Niebhur's longer version of the prayer goes like this:

God, give me grace to accept with serenity
the things that cannot be changed,
Courage to change the things
which should be changed,
and the Wisdom to distinguish
the one from the other.

Living one day at a time,
Enjoying one moment at a time,
Accepting hardship as a pathway to peace,
Taking, as Jesus did,
This sinful world as it is,

Not as I would have it,
Trusting that You will make all things right,
If I surrender to Your will,
So that I may be reasonably happy in this life,
And supremely happy with You forever in the next. Amen.

If ever there was a time to pray the serenity prayer, it is now. In our current situation, there is so little in our lives we can actually control. Against the backdrop of volatility and division, serenity distinguishes itself as a priceless, treasured keepsake.

Serenity. Acceptance. Courage. Wisdom.

In this apocalypse in which we find ourselves, may we tie our chariots to those four horsemen. Amen?

98

On a warm autumn day in 2004, our neighbor, Jack (an officer in the U S Army and a high school classmate of our oldest daughter), was killed in Iraq. The news blanketed our neighborhood and the entire city of Naperville, Illinois with sadness. This twenty-one-year-old with so much potential would return home to waiting pallbearers instead of a hero's welcome.

I grabbed some paper and a pen and scratched out a thank-you note to a brave son of his Uncle Sam:

I cried the day I heard you died.
As your flag-covered casket
was carried in slow-motion precision
to a waiting hearse,
my heavy heart grieved
with sighs too deep for words.
The things you fought for
are the possessions I cherish.
They are privileges
I could never afford on my own.
Freedom from fear.
Freedom from want.
Freedom of speech
and freedom to worship God.
Those are what you bequeathed to me.
A treasure chest of priceless gifts.
Because of you (and others like you),
I am wealthier than I can fully comprehend.

Still, in the end, in the pursuit of justice
(in which you gave your life),
it doesn't seem fair at all.

It didn't seem fair then and sixteen years later it doesn't seem fair now. But if you think life tends to be fair (pardon the pun), you don't know Jack.

The same person who began the 90th psalm with these words, *Lord, you have been our dwelling place throughout all generations,* would also include these words in the same passage:

All our days pass away under your wrath;
   we finish our years with a moan.
Our days may come to seventy years,
   or eighty, if our strength endures;
yet the best of them are but trouble and sorrow. (Psalm 90:9-10)

The world we inhabit is characterized by trouble and sorrow and tears and regret, as well as laughter and joy and contentment and peace. And not every person lives to be seventy or eighty. Some don't even make it to twenty-two.

Today offers each of us a reality check. Life is complicated. Humanity is flawed. Though created in God's image, we are broken people in need of a Savior. And on a day that recalls birthdays and death days, we need to be reminded that there is no better place to shelter in place than in the welcoming, comforting, ever-faithful heart of God.

99

Do you know the name Oswald J. Smith? He was the pastor of People's Church in Toronto. When I was in high school, I traveled with a choir that performed in the church he founded and at which he served for several decades.

In addition to being an influential pastor, Oswald Smith was also a hymn writer. Back in 1938, Pastor Smith published beautiful worship hymn entitled *God is Waiting in the Silence*. It expresses the thought that God is waiting, and earnestly desiring those who will respond to His loving call.

According to a hymn historian I found online: *Though there are passages in the Bible that call for sinners to trust in Christ and be saved, this song extends a call to professing Christians to get serious about living for God.*

Consider these challenging lyrics:

God is waiting in the silence,
For a heart that He can fill;
He must find it cleansed and empty,
With a spirit calm and still.
God is waiting in the silence,
Oh, to know that He is near!
Earth recedes, and heaven opens,
God is waiting, God is here.

God is waiting in the silence,
As the world goes rushing by;
Will not someone stop and listen,
Answer quickly, "Here am I"?

Recently I discovered that this little-known Gospel hymn had a
major impact on the man who would become the founder of
CRISTA Ministries based in Seattle. According to what I read, Mike
Martin was a Christian but he was a rather lukewarm one. As he
himself put it, he was "not working at it."

One day Mike was listening to a Christian station on his car radio.
Oswald Smith's song was playing. The question posed by the hymn
stopped him in his tracks: *Will not someone stop and listen, answer*
quickly, 'Here am I'?

Mike, feeling deeply convicted, spoke to the radio these words,
Lord, I'm coming now. You don't have to wait any longer.

From that day on he became an active and ardent servant of God.

Mike Martin founded a youth ministry to troubled young people in
Seattle called King's Teens. But it didn't stop there. He started a
private Christian school, a radio station, a senior-adult retirement
community, a youth camp, not to mention a relief and development
organization. Through CRISTA (originally known as King's
Garden) Mike's efforts experienced the Lord blessing and
transformed thousands of lives.

Like Mike, none of us has to wait any longer to respond to God's
call. The Lord will be the Savior of all who will call on Him in faith
(Romans 10:13), and He stands ready to direct and empower our
service through His Spirit.

100

Dr. Clark Hoffman is a resident on our campus where I work. This retired hand surgeon is amazing. In his early nineties, Clark still plays golf and tennis as well as serving as a deacon in a large Presbyterian church. Not long ago, Clark was part of a tour to the Holy Land I helped organize. His heart for God and his love for people inspire me.

During the coronavirus lockdown, Clark shared a poem with me. It was written by the cousin of one of his professors in medical school. It spoke to him and he thought it would speak to me. He was right.

Although written a very long time ago, this verse by an amateur poet is quite timely given the virus that finds many of our churches empty on Sunday mornings. It's called *Alone in Church*.

The chapel was empty. The light was quite dim.
I wondered if I could converse with Him.

From the pulpit, no voice. From the organ, no tone.
Yet a comforting presence made itself known.

I spoke not at all and heard not a sound.
But I understood clearly that He was around.

My questions seemed answered as though He had heard.
And it never required an audible word.

That poignant little verse was written by Professor Carl Dragstedt. It was the last poem this prolific poet ever penned.

That simple rhyme pictures the invitation the psalmist offers on behalf of our Creator: *Be still and know that God is God.* (Psalm 46:10)

One of the benefits of sheltering in place and being restricted from the normal activities of our daily lives is becoming reacquainted with alone time and quiet places.

Many years ago I heard Catholic theologian and author Henri Nouwen speak to a group of pastors. He encouraged us to spend more alone time with God. He challenged us to be still and quiet before Him.

This gentle man of God went on to say that initially we will become very distracted and want to return to the normal noise and activity of the day because it's not what we are accustomed to. He likened it to hearing birds hitting against the window pane of our homes. Silence can be distracting until we make peace with quiet.

Let me encourage you to take Nouwen's advice and try silence on for size. Not a long time. But a little time every day. Feet on the floor. Hands on your lap in an open position. Listening for what the Lord will say.

101

When President Trump was diagnosed with COVID, his political enemies prayed for his recovery. Vice President Biden, former President Obama, the Clintons and Nancy Pelosi all made it known that, in spite of their differences, they were praying for a good outcome healthwise.

Praying for your enemies. Now, there's a novel idea. Actually, it's not fiction at all. It's a Gospel idea.

It was Jesus who pioneered that progressive idea. It was one of the points driven home in his sermon on the mountain in Matthew 5:

43 You have heard that it was said, "Love your neighbor and hate your enemy." 44 But I tell you, love your enemies and pray for those who persecute you, 45 that you may be children of your Father in heaven. He causes his sun to rise on the evil and the good, and sends rain on the righteous and the unrighteous.46 If you love those who love you, what reward will you get? Are not even the tax collectors doing that? 47 And if you greet only your own people, what are you doing more than others? Do not even pagans do that? 48 Be perfect, therefore, as your heavenly Father is perfect. (Matthew 5:43-47)

Well, perfection is a bit more than we can expect from ourselves (imperfect as we are). I'm not capable of perfection. I know that. Neither are you. But maybe we can revise our perspective and perfect our definition of what the Lord expects from us.

Is that perfectly clear? I hope so. Perfect is hitting the bullseye. It's reaching the goal. It's adjusting your sight so that your aim is accurate.

If we understand perfection that way, being perfect is a bit more doable. Not performing perfectly, but perfectly understanding that loving God's way is different than simply doing what comes naturally.

Praying for someone who is struggling, someone who you don't agree with on issues. It's more than a loving thing to do. It's what God calls us to do.

102

Recently I was reminded of something I did about twenty-five years ago that I'm not so proud of.

I was in the gallery at a celebrity golf tournament in suburban Chicago. During the day I followed the likes of Bryant Gumbel, Ernie Banks, Digger Phelps and former Vice President Dan Quayle.

While watching Dan Quayle play, I got (what at the time I thought was) a brilliant idea. I remembered that he had embarrassed himself while in office by misspelling the word "potato."

Since the country club where the golf event was being held was in an upscale housing development, I went to one of the homes and asked if I could have a potato. With a potato and felt pen in hand, I approached Mr. Quayle between holes and asked if he'd autograph my spud.

He looked at me with a twinkle in his eye and graciously accommodated my request. I thought I'd pulled off a real coupe. I kept that signed russet on a shelf in my office until it rotted. I remember ruing the fact that I'd not had him sign a snack-size bag of potato chips instead.

But over the years, I've regretted what at the time seemed like a clever ploy. I capitalized on someone's mistake. Taking advantage of the vice president's faux pas was a faux pas on my part. What if someone had insisted on bringing up my misdeeds from the past? How would I feel about that?

Although I don't remember ever misspelling the word "potato," I am guilty of far worse. I've mashed another's reputation by peddling rumors. I've passed on half-baked ideas when I didn't take the time to research the facts and convey a more accurate description of the way things are.

Another could easy scallop me in public by calling to mind mistakes of my youth. I could probably French fry you if I had access to some of your foibles you hope your family has forgotten.

No wonder Jesus gave us the Golden Rule as a yardstick for our behavior: *Do unto others as you would have them do unto you.* That's the gold standard for living a life with fewer regrets.

Gratefully, grace is offered to cover what we can't undo. And gratefully, GRACE is a bit easier to spell than POTATO.

103

It wasn't COVID, but the scenario was eerily similar to what we've read about for the last seven months. A near-death experience would change the direction of my life. Although it was forty years ago, I remember it as if it were yesterday.

A close friend of mine was intubated and on life-support in Southern California. She had gone into anaphylactic shock and her lungs had collapsed. The doctors told her dad and mom all had been done for her that could be done and she wasn't responding as they'd hoped. Discovering they were religious people, the staff encouraged the parents of the twenty-eight-year-old to pray.

Because I was a pastor of a church in Seattle at the time, my friend's family called me to ask if members of my congregation would also pray for her recovery.

Well, God answered prayers on her behalf. Although her full recovery would take several weeks, a few days after I was notified of her critical situation, my friend turned the corner. She was taken off life-support by the end of the week and was discharged soon thereafter.

A couple months later, I flew down to see my friend and take her to the Rose Bowl game between Washington and Michigan. Although my Huskies lost 23-6, I felt I had won. Sitting next to my friend, I was oblivious to the other 100,000 spectators in the stands. My eyes were on her alone. Her near-death experience made me realize that I didn't want to spend the rest of my life without her.

Within the year, I asked Wendy to be my wife. Six months later, less than a mile from the medical center where she nearly died, we promised each other a lifetime of love until death eventually parts us.

There is a watershed verse many of us have committed to memory that underscores God's personal involvement in our lives when hope is all we have to cling to. It's a verse that celebrates God's purpose in our lives during times of crisis, doubt, discouragement, near-death or death itself.

It's found in the eighth chapter of Romans: *All things work together for the good of those who are called according to God's purpose.*

104

What is it about Fridays that finds us in a good mood?

Back when you were working, Fridays meant that you could press the pause button and take it easy for a couple days before resuming the workday grind.

Fridays were an invitation to take a breath. Even if the workload on Fridays was every bit as demanding as the other four days of the week, knowing a weekend awaited someone made the burden more bearable.

Fridays give a forward glance.
They help us look ahead.
They crown a week gone by with "let's move on!"
Each Friday grants finality
to what the week has wrought
by letting go of all that we have done.

Each Friday is a picture of
what Paul has called us to.
Not dwelling on the past, but letting go.
And then to focus on what waits
with joy for what's in store
while trusting God for details we don't know.

On the journey of life there are two types of travelers: Those who look through the windshield and those who repeatedly glance at the rearview mirror. The former focus on what's ahead. The latter are preoccupied with what they have already passed.

My great-aunt Ruby was a windshield traveler. She called herself "a tomorrow girl." Although approaching ninety, she dressed fashionably and heeded the trends. She was still vitally engaged with life and didn't want to miss out on what each day held in store.

Aunt Ruby led a grief-support group at her church in Poulsbo. Her purpose was to help family members who'd lost loved ones (like she had) keep a forward focus. To those on the verge of getting trapped in the quicksand of sorrow, she painted a picture of a hopeful future.

What was it the apostle Paul wrote? *Forgetting those things that are behind and straining toward what is ahead, I press on.*

I guess you'd call the Apostle Paul a "tomorrow guy."

105

Did you know that Canadians celebrate Thanksgiving on our Columbus Day? Since I married a woman who was born in Canada, we don't let this day pass without notice.

Even though the holiday for our neighbors to the north does not have the traditional trappings as our annual day of gratitude, it's a special day. The second Monday in October is always an occasion to greet our Canadian relatives who use the day to count their blessings.

Various nations of the world celebrate Thanksgiving Day. In Germany it's the first Sunday in October. In Grenada it's October 25 each year. In the Netherlands, it's the first Wednesday in November.

Having a set day to express thanks for blessings in our lives makes a lot of sense when it comes to framing such occasions with family traditions. But in no way should a token day of thanks take the place of practicing an attitude of gratitude every day of our lives.

The fact that different countries observe Thanksgiving on different days should be a reminder to us that being grateful is not limited to any one culture or to a particular day of the year.

There's a passage in the Old Testament that I tend to associate with Thanksgiving whenever or wherever it is celebrated. Psalm 100 celebrates God's goodness to all the nations of the earth:

Shout for joy to the LORD, *all the earth.*
2   *Worship the* LORD *with gladness;*
   come before him with joyful songs.
3 *Know that the* LORD *is God.*
   It is he who made us, and we are his[a];
   we are his people, the sheep of his pasture.

4 *Enter his gates with thanksgiving*
   and his courts with praise;
   give thanks to him and praise his name.
5 *For the* LORD *is good and his love endures forever;*
   his faithfulness continues through all generations.

How about it? Before we conclude this day and allow it to be captured by the history books, why not make a list of the ways God has been good and faithful to you in the past seven months (since COVID began to complicate our lives)? Call it mental math. Call it adding up evidences of God's faithfulness and subtracting the worries you needlessly embraced.

As the poet once said, *A day for counting blessings is a day for giving thanks as we embrace the faithfulness of God.*

106

On October 13, 2010, a billion people around the world watched on TV as thirty-three miners in Chile were rescued after having been trapped for sixty-nine days 2,300 feet underground.

Do you remember that dramatic event? Talk about sheltering in place. Oh my! What many thought to be a foregone conclusion proved to be a premature verdict. Doom and gloom gave way to joy and praise.

Being trapped in a copper mine is one thing. But there are other ways we can become trapped. We can become trapped in a door-less/windowless cave of being critical. Thinking negatively is a rut that is hard to get out of.

Today we can choose to be positive (even though it may not be our natural bent). Being judgmental can become so automatic that we don't even realize we are predisposed to judging another. Predisposed judging is called what? That's right! It's called Prejudice!

It is so easy for past experiences or family biases and inbred influences to overly influence the way we relate to opportunities or individuals that represent growth potential.

I have a friend whose initial response to an invitation to do something new is "no." No matter what it is, I can guarantee what he will say when posed an opportunity. It's so predictable, it's almost funny. But it's not funny. It's sad.

Trapped in the confines of what is comfortable, my friend would rather breathe the stale air of convenience than make the effort to learn or try or do something new.

Christopher Robin had a friend like my friend. Eeyore was that old gray stuffed donkey who was generally characterized as a pessimistic, gloomy and depressed. The Eeyores of this world are trapped in a cave of negativity when they could choose to be rescued for a life of positive possibility.

What was it the apostle Paul said to the church members in Philippi? His memorable words are found in chapter four of Philippians. I like the way The Message renders them:

Summing it all up, friends, I'd say you'll do best by filling your minds and meditating on things true, noble, reputable, authentic, compelling, gracious – the best, not the worst; the beautiful, not the ugly; things to praise, not things to curse. Put into practice what you learned from me, what you heard and saw and realized. Do that, and God, who makes everything work together, will work you into his most excellent harmonies. (Philippians 4:8-9)

107

John Wooden (the Wizard of Westwood) was born in the little town of Martinsville, Indiana just nineteen years after the game of basketball was invented.

As an eight-year-old, young John stuffed rags in his mother's stockings and took shots aiming at a tomato basket his father had nailed to the side of a barn.

Coach John Wooden would lead his UCLA Bruins to ten NCAA national championships in a twelve-year period. That included a record seven national championships in a row. Wooden would never underestimate the importance of discipline and practicing the essentials of the game.

One of the highlights of my freelance writing career was the privilege of interviewing Coach Wooden. Without apology, he voiced his love for his Savior. He compared his walk with the Lord to his decades-old marriage to his wife, Nellie. He told me that, although both relationships required hard work, the benefits were more than worth it.

Coach Wooden also shared with me that his faith motivated him to treat his players and colleagues with a degree of understanding that was beyond his own natural ability. By learning to accept people and circumstances he didn't fully agree with, he was able to act in ways he would not later regret.

John Wooden died just four months shy of his 100th birthday. Still the legacy he left continues to inspire people like me. Hopefully, you too. Consider these words from 1 Corinthians 9:

24 Do you not know that in a race all the runners run, but only one gets the prize? Run in such a way as to get the prize.25 Everyone who competes in the games goes into strict training. They do it to get a crown that will not last, but we do it to get a crown that will last forever. 26 Therefore I do not run like someone running aimlessly; I do not fight like a boxer beating the air. 27 No, I strike a blow to my body and make it my slave so that after I have preached to others, I myself will not be disqualified for the prize.

108

In the fall of 1993, the Nobel Peace Prize was awarded to two men. Believe it or not, one of the recipients had spent twenty-seven years in prison and was released only three and a half years earlier. If you're thinking I'm referring to Nelson Mandela, you're absolutely right.

The other recipient was Frederick de Klerk. The committee awarded the prize to these two men in recognition of their work for the peaceful termination of the apartheid regime in South Africa and laying the foundations for a new democratic government.

A black man and a white man receiving gold medallions. Those colors aren't the favorite ones typically chosen by preschoolers reaching into a box of Binney and Smith crayolas. But those are the colors that are on God's artist palette. God's gold standard for beauty is a world in which blacks and whites see each other as equals and judge one another by the content of their character.

In the past year we lost two individuals who represent champions of peace and human rights in our nation: Congressman John Lewis and Justice Ruth Bader Ginsberg. Although they did not win Nobel Peace Prizes, they won our hearts. They modeled for us the kind of tenacious perseverance required to undo unjust laws peacefully.

In Psalm 34:14 we read these words: *Turn from evil and do good. Seek peace and pursue it.*

109

The challenges of the coronavirus have hit every element of our society. Social distancing, sheltering at home and wearing face masks have become predictable protocols for every age group.

Restrictions on doing business-as-usual have hit schools, local shops and restaurants big time. But the bigger cost is an emotional one.

The American Psychological Association has found that nearly 80% of all adults indicate the current pandemic is a significant source of stress. In a recent interview with NBC News, Paul Gionfriddo, president and CEO of Mental Health America, attested to the fact that unprecedented numbers are dealing with anxiety and depression.

But among senior adults, the emotional toll is particularly taxing. Inability to see family on a regular basis in order to minimize infection has created a chronic sense of sorrow.

Lack of hugs from grandchildren feels like being sentenced to solitary confinement.

I recently reflected on the challenges impacting our residents in our staff newsletter. Making a play on our company name, I called my thoughts "COVID Living." But there is nothing playful about the impact our seniors are experiencing.

It is personally painful to watch residents struggle whose mates live in a different level of care. Restricted access to their husbands and wives results in a gnawing despair. One woman confessed her anger to me because of having to wear a mask in the presence of her husband who is hearing impaired and relies on reading lips. Another admitted to the frustration of sitting six feet apart, unable to hold hands while visiting.

But there is joy as well. I helped another woman find a spot outside her husband's second-floor window so she could converse with the love of her life on a smartphone while seeing his face.

Another cost associated with the coronavirus is the inability to celebrate the life of friends and family following their death. Public memorial services and burials are limited to small gatherings. Not having the chance to say goodbye or experience closure in grief adds to one's sorrow.

As I've observed seniors dealing with the ongoing issues associated with the pandemic, there are practical ways of combating the loneliness that seems universal. These suggestions comprise an acronym for COVID:

Creative contact. Look for fun ways to stay connected to loved ones. FaceTime with your grandchildren. Schedule in-person visits with adult children where you can communicate while remaining socially distanced.

Online worship. Take advantage of this unique opportunity to gather with your own community of faith while watching services from home. In addition, why not explore from the comfort of your family room how other churches and synagogues across the country are worshiping?

Virtual meetings. Learn how to use ZOOM so you can participate in alumni reunions, service club gatherings and book groups.

Internet entertainment. Rather than watching nonstop cable news on TV, use your computer to click on YouTubes featuring your favorite musical artists or to play online solitaire or Scrabble.

Domestic catch up. This time in which we are encouraged to stay home is a perfect time to attend to projects around the house that you've been procrastinating doing. Scrapbooking, cleaning out the garage, or cooking ahead for the holidays are a few possibilities.

110

Consider the importance of sheltering in place when the world is spinning out of control. For Noah and his family, the months they spent holed up in a "floating zoo" provided them the opportunity to distance themselves from the contagious corruption from which they could not easily escape.

Scripture tells us that it rained for forty days and forty nights. But have you ever calculated how long Noah and his family were quarantined on the ark? In the research I've done, it appears to be anywhere from 150 days to 360 days. We can relate, right? Our campus has been restricted for the better part of a year. In a very real sense, the campus where I work has been an ark in the midst of a global pandemic.

For Noah the ark was an escape. It was a refuge. It was a floating sanctuary. It was a bubble that guaranteed protection. It was a shelter that promised hope.

We all long for arks in different shapes and sizes. We desire set-apart locations where we can press the pause button and remember who we are called to be.

Sacred space where grace can breathe.
Holy ground where hope is found.
The perfect place provided by a life-sustaining God.
A lean-to on a mountain trail.
A naturally air-conditioned cave in the desert.
A treehouse in a forested jungle.

An ark on a never-ending sea.
An elegant mansion.
A modest home.
An adequate apartment.
A room with a bed.
A room with a view.
A room that (with or without windows) provides
the perspective (too-often forgotten)
of what God is saving me from
and what God is saving me for.

As challenging and as inconvenient it has been to stay at home to stay healthy, we've been given a chance to gain perspective. The ark provided Noah a chance to gain perspective about just how godless the globe had become. Sheltering in place allowed Noah quiet time to contemplate more than the cooing of the doves and the mooing of the cows. It provided him distance from the competing voices of those who had flooded the world with their flagrant sins (thumbing their noses at their Creator).

One of the benefits of a time like this is to take stock of the world around us. Reading the paper, watching the news, looking at Facebook, listening to the radio or your favorite podcast. It is no secret that our country is on a collision course with a moral recession.

Our restricted activities and limited exposure is "ark-like" in that it is allowing us the means to contemplate God's presence and God's promises as well as God's expectations of us as His people. So, what should we be doing while distancing? How should we be making the most of sheltering in place?

Trust in the Lord with all your heart. Don't lean on your own understanding. In all your ways, acknowledge Him and He will direct your paths. (Proverbs 3:5-6)

111

In the winter of 2019, Wendy and I joined the President of Covenant Living, Terri Cunliffe, and her husband, Dave, and forty other residents from our Covenant Living campuses on the west coast. We stood on top of Mount Carmel. It was thrilling.

A statue of Elijah punctuated the point where the prophet challenged the four hundred prophets of Baal and won. Having defeated the arrogant pagan priests at their own game, Elijah brought glory to Israel's God and won over the hearts of the people.

But then we find this champion of truth running for his life. He's exhausted, discouraged and in a prison of his emotions. Perhaps you've experienced a similar syndrome where after an emotional high you've tumbled into the basement of despair.

Spiritual victories can often be followed by intense times of temptation. The emotional release of adrenalin can leave a vacuum that sadness, doubt and despair can fill. From what I see in the biblical text, Elijah is suffering from depression.

When the goal you achieve
finds you claiming success
and you bask in a mountain top high,
be prepared for what's next.
Clouds of joy can bring rain.
And before long you just want to die.

From the heights to the depths.

And in no time you fall
into quicksand that robs you of breath.
There appears no escape.
Daily life is a drudge.
You're alive but it feels more like death.

Depression finds ways
to hold hostage your heart.
It brings the dark night of the soul.
Without hope you feel lost
(if you can feel at all).
The darkness of doubt takes a toll.

Elijah, after winning the Super Bowl, Stanley Cup and the World Series all put together, wanted to die. He was suicidal. He didn't want to live any longer. But he didn't need to die. He just needed to rest.

If you've ever been diagnosed with clinical depression you relate to Elijah's situation. The black dog is chasing you relentlessly down a dark alley to a dead end. The black dog. That's a great metaphor. It's how Winston Churchill described his own battle with depression.

I have felt the hot unwanted breath of that big black dog on my neck. Thirty years ago I hit the wall and wasn't sure I wanted to go on. The lights went out. I stumbled around in the darkness. I needed a guide. And gratefully God provided one. A Christian counselor helped me navigate my way back.

Like Elijah I needed to rest. That's what my therapist prescribed. Plenty of rest. Like the prophet, I had been running too fast for too long. I'd grown addicted to my own adrenalin and now was paying the price.

One of the consequences of the coronavirus is burn out and emotional exhaustion. Feeling down due to the long-term effects of

228

this pandemic is normal in this anything-but-normal season. Our emotions play havoc with us. Our joy meter is on the fritz. More often than not, we find ourselves feeling flat.

The account of Elijah reminds us that God knows how to find us and He knows how to fix us. The prophet needed plenty of rest. And he needed nourishment. And God provided just what was needed before Elijah was ready for his next assignment. For Elijah, sheltering in place was a gift in disguise. It could very well be that for us, too.

The Lord is my shepherd ... He makes lie down in green pastures ... (Psalm 23:1)

112

Did you know how old Daniel was when he was thrown into the den of lions? Scholars tend to think he was in his eighties. In a real sense, ol' Daniel (literally old Daniel) was sheltering in place. All alone. Away from the crowd. Victimized by more than a life-threatening virus, threatened by sure death, Daniel confidently trusted God for what was about to play out.

Well, as we know, Daniel's life is spared. God supernaturally kept the beasts at bay. Although the Blue-Plate Special had appeared to be "Prime Rib of Prophet," the lions were in for a big surprise. And the bottom line? The lions' share was anything but a prophet.

This past week I enjoyed a little time at recess on my favorite playground. I love to play with words. And so I went searching for words that fit the tune of "Danny Boy." It seemed like an appropriate tune while reflecting on Daniel's enforced quarantine.

Here's what I came up with:

The lions' den is where the prophet sheltered.
Against his will, he looked to God and prayed.
He knew that death was likely if not certain.
Daniel had faith and thus was not afraid.
But come the morning when the king inquired.
He heard the news he hoped somehow was true.
The prophet left his prison of sure torture.
He testified to what his God could do.

Here are a couple takeaways from this familiar story I first heard in Sunday school as the teacher moved paper figures around on a flannelgraph board. One is the fact that Daniel entered the cave of the carnivores convinced his life was in God's hands. If God wanted to take his life, that was God's prerogative. If God wanted to frustrate the king's edict and muzzle the lions, Daniel was convinced God would have His way.

But what accounted for Daniel's confidence while sheltering in place in the lions' den? That's the second takeaway. It was his practice of a life of prayer while sheltering in place in his home all those years previously. Daniel's discipline of praying three times a day resulted in a relationship with his Creator that found the prophet assured God was in control.

What a great reminder for us of the importance of prayer. Spending time with the Lord on a regular basis prepares us in advance for those times of trial when we have no choice but to trust God.

The prayer of a righteous man is powerful and effective. (James 5:16)

113

The Greek word translated "repent" in the New Testament means "to change your mind and go the other way." If you use a GPS device in your car or rely on a Google map app on your smartphone, you understand that root meaning of repenting.

When you've made a wrong turn or gone too far without taking an exit, you hear that voice say, *Proceed to the route!* or *Redirecting!*

God loves us too much to simply let us barrel full-speed-ahead when the destination to which we are headed is fraught with calamity or unnecessary complications. The Holy Spirit is that GPS mechanism that addresses our misdirection and seeks to redirect us.

Jonah learned that first hand. His U-turn was more dramatic than most. God arranged for a large fish to serve as the reluctant prophet's place of shelter. In a sense, God gave his disobedient child a "time out." My three-year-old granddaughter hates getting sent to her room or forced to sit in a corner. But it accomplishes her parents' purpose in challenging her willfulness.

Life has a way of giving us "time outs." Let me identify a few of these capsules of confinement. Unexpected unemployment. That's definitely a time-out sheltering-in-place opportunity.

So are chemotherapy treatments.

Being on the unwanted end of a painful divorce is a time-out opportunity.

When your mate of sixty years leaves you through the door of death, that opens the door to a time-out basement.

How about a relapse that leads to an inpatient treatment program?

Maybe it's as benign as a three-month round-the-world cruise following retirement.

For some it is that mandatory quarantine requirement when you've tested positive for COVID and though you are asymptomatic, you have to shelter in place alone.

All that to say, there are times in our lives when we are given the opportunity to consider where we are headed and calculate necessary course corrections. It's a timeout with a purpose. Or should I say, it's a timeout with the possibility of it being purposeful?

The prayer that Jonah prays from the belly of the fish is instructive for us in whatever place we find ourselves sheltering:

I said, "I have been banished from your sight; yet I will look again toward your holy temple. The engulfing waters threatened me, the deep surrounded me; seaweed was wrapped around my head. To the roots of the mountains I sank down; the earth beneath barred me in forever. But you, LORD my God, brought my life up from the pit. When my life was ebbing away, I remembered you, LORD, and my prayer rose to you, to your holy temple." (Jonah 2:4-7)

114

In a cell for who knows how long?
You're not guilty, but who cares?
From how it seems, nobody (even God).
You're a victim and you know it.
You're denied what you deserve.
You've been framed by those who swore you broke the law.

When you're wrongfully imprisoned
cause the system let you down,
it is easy to give up and doubt your hope.
There's no use for being hopeful
when blind justice cannot see
that the scales she holds are rigged.
How can you cope?

Good question. The headlines remind us on a regular basis that innocent people are denied justice and jailed for something they didn't do. Death rows are occupied by people who don't deserve to be there. Gratefully we are hearing more and more about organizations that are taking up the cause of those wrongly convicted.

Paul and his colleague, Silas, were incarcerated in the Macedonian city of Philippi unjustly. They got "sent up" without a trial for "standing up" for a righteous cause. In the words of John Lewis, the late Congressman from Georgia, Paul and Silas were jailed for getting into "good trouble." Good trouble! I like that, don't you?

The cell in which they were imprisoned found Paul and Silas sheltering in grace. In spite of mistreatment and injustice, they were praying and singing hymns. In other words, they were looking to God for justice and freedom. Times of quarantine can refocus our perspective in a Godward direction.

There's a passage in 1 Peter chapter 3 that really captures Paul and Silas' experience. Even more, these verses invite us trust God when things happen to us that we don't deserve:

13 Now, who will want to harm you if you are eager to do good? 14 But even if you suffer for doing what is right, God will reward you for it. So don't worry or be afraid of their threats.15 Instead, you must worship Christ as Lord of your life. And if someone asks about your hope as a believer, always be ready to explain it. 16 But do this in a gentle and respectful way.[c]Keep your conscience clear. Then if people speak against you, they will be ashamed when they see what a good life you live because you belong to Christ. 17 Remember, it is better to suffer for doing good, if that is what God wants, than to suffer for doing wrong! (1 Peter 3:13-17)

115

While driving to Tahoma National Cemetery a few weeks back, I passed a megachurch. A big signboard at the entrance announced Easter in October. Initially, it caught me off guard. But as I pondered what I saw, it made sense.

Traditional Easter services had been canceled at the church property six months earlier. COVID restrictions had prevented congregations from gathering in person. But now that protocols were permitting reduced numbers of congregants to assemble on Sundays to worship, the staff of this church wanted to provide members an Easter celebration.

And why not? The message was still valid. The reality of the resurrection had not dissipated. Now that there were tangible measures to mitigate against infection spread, it was game time. The more I thought about it, it was not unlike the NBA taking a three-month hiatus. The season was suspended until it was safe to resume play.

I decided we should follow suit at our retirement community. Even though we were not able to assemble in person, the thrust of our virtual service on All Saints Sunday (the first Sunday in November) was Easter.

As is our tradition, we remembered those residents who died during the previous year. We read their names, projected their pictures and reflected on their lives. We expressed gratitude for their faith and the promise of a reunion to come.

All Saints Sunday is a most appropriate day to celebrate the central message of the Christian faith:

… that Christ died for our sins according to the Scriptures, that he was buried, that he was raised on the third day according to the Scriptures … (1 Corinthians 15:3-4)

For Jesus, a borrowed grave in which he sheltered in place for three days, proved to be the ultimate example of sheltering in grace. That tomb is where grace showed up big time and redeemed our places of confinement in temporary capsules of faith. What Jesus accomplished by defeating death, transforms dreaded dungeons into waiting rooms. The resurrection is more than a promissory note redeemable upon death. It is God's way of saying that dead ends and sealed-off caves this side of Heaven are not ultimate destinations.

116

When I was in seminary in Southern California, I attended Hollywood Presbyterian Church. My pastor was Dr. Lloyd Ogilvie (who would eventually become chaplain of the United States Senate). Lloyd would begin each Sunday morning worship with these words: *The living Christ is here!* It was more than a subtle reminder that every Sunday was Easter Sunday.

Speaking of Easter, the whole concept of sheltering in place finds me picturing Mary Magdalene as she left the garden tomb following her unexpected encounter with Jesus that first Easter morning. I'm guessing she was walking on air (even as she ran to tell the disciples her amazing experience).

And where does Mary find her grieving friends? That's right! They were sheltering in place. There's another phrase with which we have become very familiar in recent weeks. Only for them it wasn't "stay at home to stay healthy." It was "stay put to stay alive."

The Easter text says they were behind locked doors. Their self-enforced quarantine was due to the fact that they were afraid. The fear from which they cowered was not related to an invisible pandemic. Rather, it was fear of those who had put Jesus to death who might come looking for them too.

But Jesus intercepted their fears by meeting them at the intersection of what they feared might happen and what they hoped would happen.

Here's the take-away. The risen Christ wants to assure those he loves that they matter to him. Christ has been raised from the dead not just to add a line to the Apostle's Creed. He lives to impact our lives with meaning, significance and joy.

Where do you find yourself today? In a garden alone *grieving?* At home with a handful of friends *fearing?* On a hospital bed in hospice care *waiting?* Reading an email from a family member *crying?* Jesus knows how to surprise us and remind us we are not forgotten.

And because Jesus carries on this mission invisibly, he uses people like you and me to represent him.

117

A few years ago I was asked to speak at a regional conference of church librarians. My assigned topic was grief.

I guess there was an assumption that a chaplain at a retirement community would know something about grief. They must have figured that anyone with a job description that consists of helping people pack their bags for heaven would know something about it. And they were correct! Grief shows up in my office on a regular basis. Often without an appointment.

As I prepared to speak at the conference, I reflected on how grief impacts us. How it sucks our joy like a leach and sends its tentacles down deep. Grief can't be gotten rid of easily or quickly. In my journal, I wrote:

Grief is that thistle in your heart
that can't be tweezered out.
It burns with such intensity
and fills your mind with doubt.

Its ache just will not go away.
Sometimes you want to die.
It leaves you wrestling your faith
and questioning God 'why?'

Grief's stubborn itch cannot be scratched.
It just won't go away.
It robs your joy and steals your smile
and colors your world gray.

And worst of all, few understand
what you are going through
unless by death, divorce or loss
grief's thistle found them, too.

But can good come out of grief? Can joy come out of sorrow?

We are taking part in an ongoing experiment right now, aren't we? The coronavirus has caused grief and sorrow (not to mention anxiety and fear) in addition to inconvenience and social distancing.

But looking back can we agree that there are positive consequences to such a negative crisis? A Capuchin Franciscan monk in Ireland wondered the same thing. His poem, *Lockdown,* went viral shortly after the pandemic went global. Me thinks it worth reading and re-reading:

All over the world people are slowing down and reflecting.
All over the world people are looking at their neighbors in a new way.
All over the world people are waking up to a new reality...
to how big we really are,
to how little control we really have,
to what really matters, to Love.

So we pray and we remember that:
Yes, there is fear.
But, there does not have to be hate.
Yes, there is isolation.
But, there does not have to be loneliness.
Yes, there is panic buying.
But, there does not have to be meanness.
Yes, there is sickness.
But, there does not have to be disease of the soul
Yes, there is even death.
But, there can always be a rebirth of love.

Wake to the choices you make as to how to live now.
Today, breathe.
Listen! Behind the factory noises of your panic
the birds are singing again.
The sky is clearing.
Spring is coming.
And we are always encompassed by Love.
Open the windows of your soul
and (though you may not be able
to touch across the empty square), sing!

118

On May 18, 1980 at 8:32 a.m., a sudden 5.1 magnitude earthquake and eruption rocked beautiful Mount Saint Helens in Washington State.

The north side of the peak rippled and blasted out ash at 650 miles per hour. A cloud of ash, rocks, gas and glacial ice roared down the side of the mountain at 100 mph. Fourteen miles of the Toutle River were buried up to 150 feet deep in the debris. Magma, at 1,300 degrees Fahrenheit, flowed for miles.

Millions of trees were scorched and burned by the hot air alone. When the glacier atop the mountain melted, a massive mudslide wiped out homes and dammed up rivers throughout the area.

The plume of ash belched out for nine hours; winds carried it across the state and as far away as Minnesota. The falling ash clogged carburetors and thousands of motorists were stranded. Fifty-seven people died overall from suffocation, burns and other assorted injuries.

Twenty-seven bodies, including that of the stubborn Harry Truman who refused to evacuate his cabin, were never found. Mount St. Helens went from 9,600 feet high to only 8,300 feet high in a matter of seconds.

Twenty-five years later, Mount St. Helens was in the news again. There were concerns that she might blow her top (what little top she had left). But that wasn't the only major event that was making news in 2005. The Iraq War, Hurricane Katrina, bird flu and mad cow disease were also on the front page. There was so much going on that seemed apocalyptic; I waxed poetic in my blog.

Here's what I wrote:

There're wars, earthquakes and tidal waves.
Then deadly aftershocks.
Could Armageddon be on deck?
So ask newsmen on Fox.

And hurricanes are on the rise
with killer floods in tow.
There's talk of bird flu and mad cow.
St. Helens's set to blow.

A Carpenter from Nazareth
once hammered home the truth
that escalating tragedies
would wake prophetic sleuths.

So could the end be drawing close
for late great planet Earth?
Are all these headlines labor pains
that mark redemption's birth?

We can't be sure, but let's beware.
The Scriptures make it clear.
That Carpenter will come again.
Perhaps this is the year.

Given the confluence of recent cataclysmic events, Christians are wondering if the current signs of the times are pointing to the soon return of Christ. Do COVID, global warming, the threat of nuclear war, unstable weather patterns, devastating earthquakes and mass shootings point in that direction?

Our personal lives are often on the verge of volcanic eruption. Without warning, the molten lava of heartbreaking news leaves us languishing. But don't despair. We have reason to hope.

The words of the psalmist in Psalm 46 celebrate the truth of God's ability to protect those who are in need of sheltering in place:

God is our refuge and strength, an ever-present help in trouble. Therefore, we will not fear, though the earth give way and the mountains fall into the heart of the sea though its waters roar and foam and the mountains quake with their surging. (Psalm 46:1-2)

119

Prior to his ascension, Jesus instructed his disciples to return to Jerusalem and wait for a gift the Father would bestow on them. The next several days of confinement in that familiar upper room culminated in baptism of the Holy Spirit. That baptism inaugurated a movement on the face of the earth that refused to be snuffed out. In fact, persecutions and trials have only served to fertilize the growth of the Kingdom of God.

It was an early church father by the name of Tertullian who said, *The blood of the martyrs became the seed of the church.*

The Bible is replete with illustrations of how God used unanticipated times of hardship to soften the hearts of his servants. The pages of God's Word are filled with reference after reference of individuals who were placed on unpaid leave or sheltered in place as a way of accomplishing God's purpose for their lives and His ultimate plan.

Dr. David Jeremiah, the senior pastor of Shadow Mountain Community Church in suburban San Diego, has chronicled some of these rather well-known examples of quarantine:

God sheltered Noah and his family for one year in the ark until Noah emerged to become the father of all the nations of the world.

God sheltered Jacob in the home of his uncle Laban when he needed to escape the wrath of Esau, his brother. And twenty years later Jacob emerged with a new family, new wealth and a new identity. He became Israel. The new name for God's chosen people.

246

God sheltered Joseph from his seventeenth year to his thirtieth. But his slavery and imprisonment became the school where God prepared him for greatness.

God sheltered Moses in a remote desert for forty years, but Moses came forth to liberate the Jewish people from Egypt.

God sheltered Naomi in the barren land of Moab until she nearly became bitter. But she and her daughter-in-law, Ruth, traveled to Bethlehem to participate in one of the greatest love stories of history.

The pastor goes on to talk about Jonah and Elijah and David and Daniel and how each of them being sheltered in place brought about unexpected amazing results that contributed to God's work in the world.

David Jeremiah identifies how the apostle Paul was quarantined in a Roman jail, but that from his house arrest came four amazing letters that are part of the New Testament.

He describes how the apostle John was confined to the island of Patmos as a prisoner but used his solitary confinement to write the Book of Revelation.

A person really could do a case study on how God throughout history has redeemed sheltering-in-place situations to bring about unimaginable outcomes that are exceedingly more abundant than we could ask for or conceive of.

What was it that Paul said? *All things work together for good to them who are called according to God's purposes.* (Romans 8:28)

What does that mean, anyway? It means that God is not put off by the problems or predicaments or pandemics of our lives. Our sovereign Creator creates possibilities within situations that seem impossible. He orchestrates opportunities from misfortune. He turns cabin fever into the warm glow of His presence. Unintended shelters become sanctuaries.

120

For me the twenty-third psalm pulls back the curtain, revealing a picture of paradise. It's a portrait of contentment. *The Lord is my shepherd. I shall not want.*

It's an invitation to renewal and rest. *He makes me lie down. He restores my soul.*

It's a celebration of beauty and wonder. *Green pastures. Still waters.*

Doesn't it do your heart good to know that the One who is our shepherd is a God who delights in what delights us? Green pastures. Still waters. Flowery meadows. Flashing seas. Brilliant sunrises. Awesome sunsets. Mountain vistas and high deserts.

Ours is a God of beauty and wonder. Magnificence and artistry. Our God is a poet whose spoken word calls worlds and stars into existence in symmetry and order. No wonder we long for paradise. It's part of our DNA. We resonate with the "awe" of awesome.

But what are we to make of the death valleys that we encounter? Shadow-covered valleys across which we are forced to journey? *Yea, though I walk through the valley of the shadow of death …*

Even with the Creator of beauty at our side as our shepherd, there are times when our eyes are blind to the wonders that surround us. There are times we feel the chill caused by the shadows as we attempt to navigate Death Valley.

Notice that the psalmist doesn't say if I walk through the valley of the shadow of death. He says "THOUGH I walk..." It's not "if." It's "when."

Some might say this pandemic is a valley of the shadow of death. What else would you call 150,000 deaths in the course of five months? Oh, my gosh! Back in March when the MLB spring training was abruptly canceled, we had no idea that being stranded at first would give way to sheltering at home.

When life blindsides us with unanticipated crises, we have a choice. We can question the existence of God or we can affirm our faith in God.

The psalmist chose to affirm his faith in the Shepherd. I just love this about the fourth verse in Psalm 23. David goes from referring to God in the third person *"The Lord* is my Shepherd ... *He* ..."* to referring to God in the second person *"Thou* are with me ..."* *"Thy* rod and *thy* staff ..."*

In the midst of hardship, his heart is softened toward the Lord. He discovers an intimacy he has not known before. A distant God becomes the psalmist's personal shepherd.

I also note that David doesn't sugarcoat what's going on around him. He doesn't deny the facts. It's not fake news. There is a problem. He calls it EVIL.

There is evil in our world, but David refuses to be sucked into a vortex of fear. He acknowledges what is happening. He knows it is beyond his ability to control it. But what does he say? *"I will fear no evil."*

And the reason he chose not to give in to his fears or doubts was the confidence he had that his Shepherd was still at his side even as he recognized the enemies bearing down on him.

It's the Shepherd who is caring for him in tangible ways all the while he is surrounded by circumstances in his life that render him vulnerable.

The psalm recognizes that life is a journey. It's more like a 26.2-mile marathon than a 100-yard dash. But along the journey the Shepherd promises a couple sheep dogs to nip at our heels, keeping us on the trail. Their names? Goodness and Mercy! Our loving Shepherd wants to make sure we are heading in the right direction on our way home.

Goodness and mercy shall follow me all the days of my life. (Psalm 23:6)

121

Praise the Lord! Have you ever noticed that Psalm 150 begins and ends with the same three words?

It's a command. It's what we are to do every day of our lives. We are commanded to affirm God's goodness against the backdrop of how bad things might be. And who would have guessed when we ushered in 2020 that a year whose name suggested perfect vision, would end up being a blur of news headlines chronicling coronavirus, COVID-related deaths, police brutality, peaceful protests, bloody riots and virtual worship services and virtual classrooms?

Being commanded to praise the Lord, is to assert what we know to be true about God in spite of how horrific or hard life seems to be. In spite of how sick we feel. In spite of how far our family members live from us. In spite of how far we feel from God. In spite of how dark the future seems.

But, now hear this! In spite of our tendency to be verbally challenged in finding words with which to praise God, we can always manage to tell the Lord we love Him.

Several years ago I was in the gallery at a Senior PGA golf tournament. For part of the day I followed Tom Lehman, a former captain of the US Ryder Cup and an outspoken follower of Jesus. As Tom walked by me headed to the next tee, I noticed a little boy come up to him and say, *How's it goin', Dad?*

It was Tom Lehman's son. The two exchanged a few words and then the boy said, *I love you, Dad.* And Tom responded with *I love you, too, son!*

In the midst of doing his job, this dad was not bothered by his son's interruption. If anything, it reminded him why he was doing his job.

It was a picture to me of my relationship with my Heavenly Father. As His son, I know God is never too busy to be reminded how much I love Him.

In Psalm 150 the psalmist gives us a tangible clue as to where we can express our love to the Lord. He writes:
Praise God in His sanctuary.

So, where is the nearest sanctuary? Among other things, the coronavirus has expanded our understanding of what a sanctuary looks like. Obviously, it means formal places set aside for worship. Settings like Gothic cathedrals, stone chapels and store-front churches. But it can also mean multipurpose rooms, living rooms, family rooms, patios and parking lots.

You get the picture. COVID has taught us that a sanctuary is not limited to a place punctuated by pews in a church building. Sanctuaries are where we verbalize our love for our Heavenly Father.

122

I lift up my eyes to the hills! Where will my help come from? (Psalm 120:1)

When you and I first learned Psalm 121, we more than likely learned it this way: *I lift up my eyes to the hills from whence cometh my help.*

That's how the King James Version renders it. That rendering suggests it's the hills that surrounded the psalmist that were symbols of much-needed strength. But translators later discovered that was not a good rendering of the Hebrew. The psalmist really wrote something more like this:

I lift my eyes to the mountains! Where will my help come from?

In other words, the mountains (as majestic and dominating and graceful and glorious as they appear from a distance) are a source of fear.

COVID is a mountain that towers over us. Death is another one of the mountains in our lives. That Rainier-size peak casts a pretty imposing shadow over our campus. The dreaded diagnosis of dementia is another mountain that dominates the horizon for many of our loved ones.

Change. Now that's another mountain in our lives. Constant change is an imposing peak that threatens all of us. We long for stability. We fear change.

But the psalmist is explicit. In uncertain times he has reason to be hopeful. He writes:

Our helps comes from the Lord who made Heaven and earth.

Some time ago I wrote a psalm that celebrates the truth of this psalm:

God remains our source of courage
when we're traumatized by terror.
When we're haunted by the headlines
and the violence everywhere.
Hear God whisper in the silence,
Don't despair, I'm in control.
Hurting hearts and broken cities
will at last one day be whole.

God can sense our anxious worry
when our hearts are filled with fear.
When an unknown virus threatens
to contaminate us here.
Then God whispers in the silence,
Do not let your fears run free.
What remains unknown to experts
is no mystery to Me.

God invites us to be trusting
when we find that faith is hard.
When we're fearful for our safety
and our nerves are frayed or jarred.
Still God whispers in the silence,
Even when your faith is weak,
I will keep your feet from stumbling
when your way is dark and bleak.

123

Epidemics and unexpected times of suffering that blindside us are opportunities in disguise. These difficult circumstances (that remind us how helpless we are in light of things that are beyond our ability to control) provide us with the chance to see God come through on our behalf.

When I was in a student at Seattle Pacific University, a young African American musician by the name of Andrae Crouch came to our campus for a concert. One of the songs he performed was one he had written. It flowed out of a time of deep despair in his personal life. He called it *Through it All*.

I've had many tears and sorrows,
I've had questions for tomorrow,
there's been times I didn't know right from wrong.
But in every situation,
God gave me blessed consolation,
that my trials come to only make me strong.

Through it all, through it all,
I've learned to trust in Jesus.
I've learned to trust in God.
Through it all, through it all,
I've learned to depend upon His Word.

But Andrae Crouch wasn't the first to discover the fact that difficult times help us discover God's grace. It was the apostle Paul who candidly admitted that when he was weak he became a candidate for divine strength. In other words, adversity made him aware of God's power in his life.

When circumstances rob us of our strength and leave us feeling totally inadequate, we don't need to cave to fear. It's okay to admit that we can't bear the weight of our anxiety on our own. Asking for help may be the bravest thing we ever do.

124

Back when COVID cast its shadow on our community, we went into lockdown to prevent infection. I wrote what I called the coronavirus checklist.

Wash your hands twelve times a day.
Stay at least six feet away.
Stay at home if you feel sick.
Sneeze into your arm.

Please avoid our nursing home.
Disinfect your mobile phone.
Isolate as best you can.
FaceTime those you love.

You can manage, yes you can.
Plan your day then work your plan.
Play it safe and safely live.
Start each day with prayer!

As we took that whimsical checklist seriously, our campus was able to remain relatively healthy. There were only about a dozen reported infections between staff and residents. Thanks to God, all of them recovered.

All the same, the words to Psalm 46 became a meaningful reminder of where our hope is found when crisis strikes. In fact, it occurred to me that the first nineteen words of Psalm 46 are an antidote to COVID (even when an effective vaccine is found).

God is our refuge and strength, an ever-present help in time of trouble.
(Psalm 46:1)

Martin Luther wrote his timeless hymn based on those inspired words. *A Mighty Fortress is Our God* reminds us of a refuge where we are always welcome to shelter in place.

But Luther is not the only one to paraphrase Psalm 46. It was the British preacher, Charles Spurgeon, who observed, "As God is all-sufficient, our defense and our might are equal to all emergencies … He is not as the swallows that leave us in the winter; He is a Friend in need, and a Friend indeed. When it is very dark with us, let brave spirits say, 'Come, let us sing the forty-sixth!'"
A fortress firm and steadfast rock, is God in time of danger;
A shield and sword in every shock, from foe well-known or stranger.

My dear friend, Bryan Jeffrey Leech, wrote a hauntingly poignant hymn that celebrates where we can shelter in grace. His lyrics were composed for the movie *The Hiding Place* that tells the inspiring story of Corrie ten Boom.

The Hiding Place
In a time of trouble, in a time forlorn,
There is a hiding place where hope is born.
In a time of danger, when our faith is proved,
There is a hiding place where we are loved.

There is a hiding place, a strong protective space,
Where God provides the grace to persevere;
For nothing can remove us from the Father's love,
Tho' all may change, yet nothing changes here.

In a time of sorrow, in a time of grief,
There is a hiding place to give relief.
In a time of weakness, in a time of fear,
There is a hiding place where God is near.

125

I love it when those who resonate with what I write share readings with me that have been meaningful to them. One such discovery was a free-verse poem written by Sarah Bourns that went viral on social media when COVID first found us sheltering in place. The poem is titled "Exposed". Her words were at once convicting and comforting.

As one who enjoys recess on a playground of words, I find Sarah's unexpected use of the word "exposed" refreshing.

We've all been exposed.
Not necessarily to the virus
(though maybe ... who knows).
We've all been exposed BY the virus.

Corona is exposing us.
Exposing our weak sides.
Exposing our dark sides.
Exposing what normally lays far beneath the surface of our souls,
hidden by the invisible masks we wear.
Now exposed by the paper masks we can't hide far enough behind.

Corona is exposing our addiction to comfort.
Our obsession with control.
Our compulsion to hoard.
Our protection of self.

Corona is peeling back our layers.
Tearing down our walls.
Revealing our illusions.
Leveling our best-laid plans.

Corona is exposing the gods we worship:
Our health
Our hurry
Our sense of security.
Our favorite lies
Our secret lusts
Our misplaced trust.

Corona is calling everything into question:
What is the church without a building?
What is my worth without an income?
How do we plan without certainty?
How do we love despite risk?

Corona is exposing me.
My mindless numbing
My endless scrolling
My careless words
My fragile nerves.

We've all been exposed.
Our junk laid bare.
Our fears made known.
The band-aid torn.
The masquerade done.

So what now? What's left?
Clean hands
Clear eyes
Tender hearts.

What Corona reveals, God can heal.

Come, Lord Jesus.
Have mercy on us.

P.S. Not until I was editing my daily meditations for publication did I discover that Sarah Bourns is part of the pastoral staff at Hope Midtown in New York City. Upon further research, I was pleased to learn that Hope Midtown is an Evangelical Covenant congregation. That's the denomination I've been part of for forty-five years. I'd call that a Godwink!

Postscript

The cover photo for this book is more than a pretty image. It was chosen specifically for this project. It portrays hope in the midst of uncertain times. The willow tree on the campus of Covenant Living at the Shores is a symbol of tenacity, perseverance and survival. Against the dark storm clouds on the horizon, that green tree that dominates our waterfront is a picture of a place to shelter. But it is more than an image on a book cover. It is a metaphor of our ultimate hope. Let me explain.

As a chaplain at a retirement community, anticipated death is a common occurrence for me. Unexpected death, on the other hand, takes my breath away. That was the situation when a dear friend and ministry colleague died while on a preaching mission in Bali. Although in his early eighties, Bud Palmberg was in relatively good health. Quite unexpectedly he lost his balance on the way to dinner, fell and hit his head. The resulting brain injury proved fatal. The emotional impact on our community was significant.

Since Bud has been a fixture in my life for forty years, his sudden death hit me harder than normal. As a fellow pastor seventeen years my senior, he mentored me when I was called to my first church out of seminary. We regularly played golf on Mondays. He even provided premarital counseling when Wendy and I got engaged.

I never could have guessed that twenty-five years later I would have the privilege of being called to lead the church in suburban Seattle he had served for a quarter of a century. Neither could I have anticipated I would be his chaplain the last several years of his life.

Dealing with my friend's unexpected death was made a bit easier knowing he was ready to go. Whereas a significant part of my job description is helping residents "pack their bags for Heaven," Bud's bags were already packed, tagged and waiting for pick up. A sermon he gave at church a year before he died called attention to his anticipation of death and his hope of resurrection. An audio clip of that sermon was played at his memorial service.

About the time Bud preached on his readiness to die, another unexpected death occurred at our retirement community. It was a giant willow tree that had guarded our lakefront for over a hundred years. This much-loved fixture to our campus had provided shade and shelter for many a church picnic, family outing or outdoor concert.

Five days following a 4th of July performance by a 75-piece community band, the tree collapsed in the middle of the night. Although we were grateful the giant willow had not fallen on any unsuspecting individuals, the shock of the tree's demise was palpable. We were grief-struck. It was like losing a friend. The sudden loss of what we had taken for granted was devastating.

The arborists were called to remove the lifeless remains. The broad outstretched limbs we had grown to love were hauled away. All that was left was an eight-foot vertical stump in the ground. It would serve as a grave marker identifying the final resting place of a friend we would miss.

Because the emotional impact could not be ignored, I decided it was appropriate to hold a memorial service for the tree. Nothing in my seminary training had prepared me for such a ceremony, but I adapted the outline I typically use for funerals.

About twenty residents joined me around the trunk. I read the twenty-third psalm. I also read the much-loved poem, "Trees," by Joyce Kilmer. We sang a hymn. I prayed a prayer of thanksgiving thanking the Lord for the memories our "friend" had left us.

In spite of the visual emptiness, there was a sense of closure. We had paid respect to part of God's creation that had beautified our campus for 110 years. But in all honesty, I continued to miss what had been and was no longer.

As I contemplated my ongoing sorrow, I understood why I felt what I did. Like all willow trees, our late friend had been a sentry. For decades it guarded our property as boats tied up on our docks and welcomed boaters as they approached our campus from the lake. But this tree was more than a silent greeter. It was a symbol of hope.

Through the years I'd learned that willow trees are the last trees to lose their yellow leaves in the fall and that they are the first trees to sprout green shoots in the spring. Against the backdrop of the beige and gray of winter, the willow quietly trumpets the arrival of new life.

With the emergence of daffodils, tulips and Easter lilies, the truth of resurrection glory is imbedded in nature. Every year as winter gives way to spring, death gives way to life. Our tree had been part of that annual pageantry. But what would take its place now that it was gone?

The next spring as I prepared to lead our annual sunrise service on the lakeshore, I walked by the stump of the old willow tree. What I saw was a source of wonder. In the dawn's early light was picture of resurrection. New life had started growing from what had died. Green shoots were emerging from the trunk. Death was being swallowed up by evidence of life.

In the months that followed, the tree continued to regenerate. It was amazing. I began to refer to this anomaly as "the resurrection tree." When I would host guests for lunch on campus, I would inevitably walk them by the tree and tell them the story.

"The resurrection tree" has become a source of comfort to me as I grieve those in my life who have been taken from me through the door of death. In addition to those residents to whom I've attended as they breathed their last, the past couple years has found me burying my mom, my sister-in-law and a forty-one-year-old nephew.

The tree on our campus is a beautiful reminder that people of faith do not grieve as those who have no hope.

Obviously, we grieve. Grief is an indicator that we have loved. Grief is proof of the fact that we have shared life and made memories with those who are significant to us. But as St. Paul reminds us, an empty first century grave empties grief of its hopelessness. I guess you could call that "good grief."

Against the dark clouds of an impending storm, that tree stands out as a silent witness. Her green branches remind us that death gives way to life. Her presence in the midst of a pandemic invites us to look beyond the present to a hopeful future.

Epilogue

A COVID Hymn

In our church on Sunday morning, we claim our place.
Social distancing's required. There's so much space.
While we long for what's familiar,
we're convinced we're loved by those here.
We're a fam'ly so we won't fear
what COVID brings.

Though we're masked our hearts are singing worshipful praise.
Empty choir lofts are sad but leave us unfazed.
When we worship God in Spirit
others have no need to hear it.
God is there in spite of COVID
evenings and days.

In the silence God is speaking. "Don't be dismayed.
COVID cannot keep Me from you. Don't be afraid."
God alone can calm our stressing
when we're candidly confessing
how we daily are distressing
distanced and stayed.

He's the vine and we're the branches nourished by grace.
We're abiding by the Spirit, sheltered in place.
In this world of tribulation,
COVID, fires and race relations,
we can trust the Lord of Nations
for what we need.

by Greg Asimakoupoulos
tune: All Through the Night

Afterword

Just as I was set to send off the manuscript of my new book to the publisher, news broke about Alex Trebek's death. Since members of our family are big *Jeopardy* watchers (from my nearly ninety-year-old father-in-law to my nearly four-year-old granddaughter), we felt like we'd lost a friend. Because Alex's death has impacted our nation in a big way, I felt like I had to write an epilogue to my book referencing it.

A Scripture passage came to mind as I pounded my keyboard reflecting on the passing of *Jeopardy's* beloved host. They were those heartfelt words from Job where he affirms his faith in the midst of adversity. I wasn't exactly sure of the chapter and verse. I knew it was something like *Even if God lets me die, I will keep trusting in Him.*

As I Googled key words, I found the verses I was looking for. Imagine my delight to find the word *jeopardy* in the text. Do I have your interest?

Here's what I wrote for the residents of our campus the day after Alex Trebek died:

It's the 9th of November and it's a Monday. Here's hoping your weekend was what you'd planned. Well, it wasn't what the Seahawks had in mind. Suffice it to say, they were Buffaloed. I'm sure it finds Pete Carroll and Russell Wilson and Monday morning quarterbacks like you and me looking for answers.

Speaking of answers. The answer is "a Canadian-born game show host who stole America's heart." Question: "Who was Alex Trebek?"

I, with you, heard the sad news about the host of Jeopardy yesterday. Oh my! We knew he was very ill. Back in the spring of 2019 he confided to his contestants and his loyal viewers that he had stage 4 pancreatic cancer. But we kept hoping Alex might beat the odds. And for a year and half, he did.

The "king of trivia" taught us that facing the future with courage is anything but a trivial pursuit. He wasn't afraid to look ahead. In spite of dark clouds of uncertainty that gathered on the horizon of his life, he kept at a job he felt destined for and entertained us night after night even as he inspired us to keep learning and increase our knowledge.

But just knowing facts is not enough. Life consists of questions and answers. So does the Bible. The book of Job is a case in point. Well-rehearsed answers don't always correlate to the questions life poses (or the ones God asks for that matter).

Faith comes to play when we think we have the right question to the obvious answer. We're all set to ring in, complete the category and add to our earnings. But much to our dismay, our buzzer doesn't work. At times like that we have no recourse but to "shelter in grace."

There is that wonderful response Job offers his critics when he feels cornered by their caustic insensitivity and (in the midst of his unimagined pain) looks toward the horizon with hope.

Keep silent and let me speak; then let come to me what may. Why do I put myself in jeopardy and take my life in my hands? Though he slay me, yet will I hope in him. (Job 13:13-15)

In other words, the answers on God's board may not always jive with our questions. Circumstances, like Job's critics might, seem unfair.

Blindsided by the apparent silence of a kind and holy God, we find ourselves (with Job) protesting against injustice. But in Job's protestations, the victim of grief's virus voices his unconditional trust in the Lord of his life.

And can we not do the same when our future seems in jeopardy? *Though he slay me, yet I will hope in him.*

I heard the executive producer of Jeopardy interviewed earlier this morning. He said that Alex's last day was spent doing what he loved. He was sitting next to his wife on their backyard swing looking at the horizon. Don't you just love that?

I believe that's what the Lord would have us do. Surround ourselves with those we love (and who love us) and face what's to come with courage and with confidence casting our cares on One who invites our unconditional trust.

About the Author

Greg Asimakoupoulos is an ordained minister and freelance writer. Over four decades, Greg has served congregations of The Evangelical Covenant Church in Washington, California and Illinois. Since 2013 he has been the fulltime chaplain at Covenant Living at the Shores.

Greg is the author of thirteen books including *The Ptarmigan Telegraph, Prayers from My Pencil, Sunday Rhymes and Reasons,* and *Finding God in 'It's a Wonderful Life'*. He is a regular columnist for three newspapers and a frequent contributor to Christian periodicals. His weekly poetic commentary (Rhymes and Reasons) can be accessed at: partialobserver.com

Greg and his wife Wendy have three grown daughters and two granddaughters. They live on Mercer Island in suburban Seattle.